Praise for the "Kids Love" Guidebook travel series

On-Air Personality Comments (Television Interviews)

"The great thing about these books is that your whole family actually lives these adventures" – (**WKRC-TV**, Cincinnati)

"Very helpful to lots of families when the kids say, I bored...and I don't want to go to same places again!" – (**WISH-TV**, Indianapolis)

"Dividing the state into many sections, the book has something for everyone...everywhere." – (**WLVT-TV**, Pennsylvania)

"These authors know first-hand that it's important to find hands-on activities that engage your children..." (**WBNS-TV**, Columbus)

"You spent more than 1000 hours doing this research for us, that's really great – we just have to pick up the book and it's done..." (**WTVR-TV**, Richmond)

"A family that's a great source for travel ideas..." (**WBRA-TV**, Roanoke)

"What a great idea...this book needed to be done a long time ago!" (**WKYT-TV**, Lexington)

"A fabulous idea...places to travel that your kids will enjoy" (**WOOD-TV**, Grand Rapids)

"The Zavatskys call it a dream come true, running their own business while keeping the family together. Their goal, encourage other parents to create special family travel memories." - (**WLVT-TV,** Pennsylvania)

"It's a wonderful book, and as someone who has been to a lot of these places...you hit it right on the money!" – (**WKRC-TV**, Cincinnati)

Praise for the "Kids Love" Guidebook travel series

Customer Comments (actual letters on file)

"I wanted to tell you how helpful all your books have been to my family of 6. I rarely find books that cater to families with kids. I have your Indiana, Ohio, Kentucky, Michigan, and Pennsylvania books. I don't want to miss any of the new books that come out. Keep up the great ideas. The books are fantastic. I have shown them to tons of my friends. They love them, too." – H.M.

"I bought the Ohio and Indiana books yesterday and what a blessing these are for us!!! We love taking our grandsons on Grammie & Papaw trips thru the year and these books are making it soooo much easier to plan. The info is complete and full of ideas. Even the layout of the book is easy to follow...I just wanted to thank you for all your work in developing these books for us..." – G.K

"I have purchased your book. My grandchildren and I have gone to many of the places listed in your book. They mark them off as we visit them. We are looking forward to seeing many more. It is their favorite thing to look at the book when they come over and find new places to explore. Thank you for publishing this book!" - B.A.

"At a retail price of under $15.00, any of the books would be well worth buying even for a one-time only vacation trip. Until now, when the opportunity arose for a day or weekend trip with the kids I was often at a loss to pick a destination that I could be sure was convenient, educational, child-friendly, and above all, fun. Now I have a new problem: How in the world will we ever be able to see and do all the great ideas listed in this book? I'd better get started planning our next trip right away. At least I won't have to worry about where we're going or what to do when we get there!" – VA Homeschool Newsletter

"My family and I used this book this summer to explore Ohio! We lived here nearly our entire life and yet over half the book we never knew existed. These people really know what kids love! Highly recommended for all parents, grandparents, etc." – Barnes and Noble website reviewer

A Parent's Guide to Exploring Fun Places in Georgia With Children...Year Round!

George & Michele Zavatsky

Dedicated to the Families of Georgia

For the latest major updates corresponding to the pages in this book visit our website:

www.KidsLoveTravel.com

- ***REMEMBER:*** *Museum exhibits change frequently. Check the site's website before you visit to note any changes. Also, HOURS and ADMISSIONS are subject to change at the owner's discretion. If you are tight on time or money, check the attraction's website or call before you visit.*
- ***INTERNET PRECAUTION:*** *All websites mentioned in KIDS LOVE GEORGIA have been checked for appropriate content. However, due to the fast-changing nature of the Internet, we strongly urge parents to preview any recommended sites and to always supervise their children when on-line.*

ISBN-13: 978-0972685467
ISBN-10: 0-972685464

KIDS ♥ GEORGIA ™ Kids Love Publications

TABLE OF CONTENTS

State Map

(With Major Routes and Cities Marked)

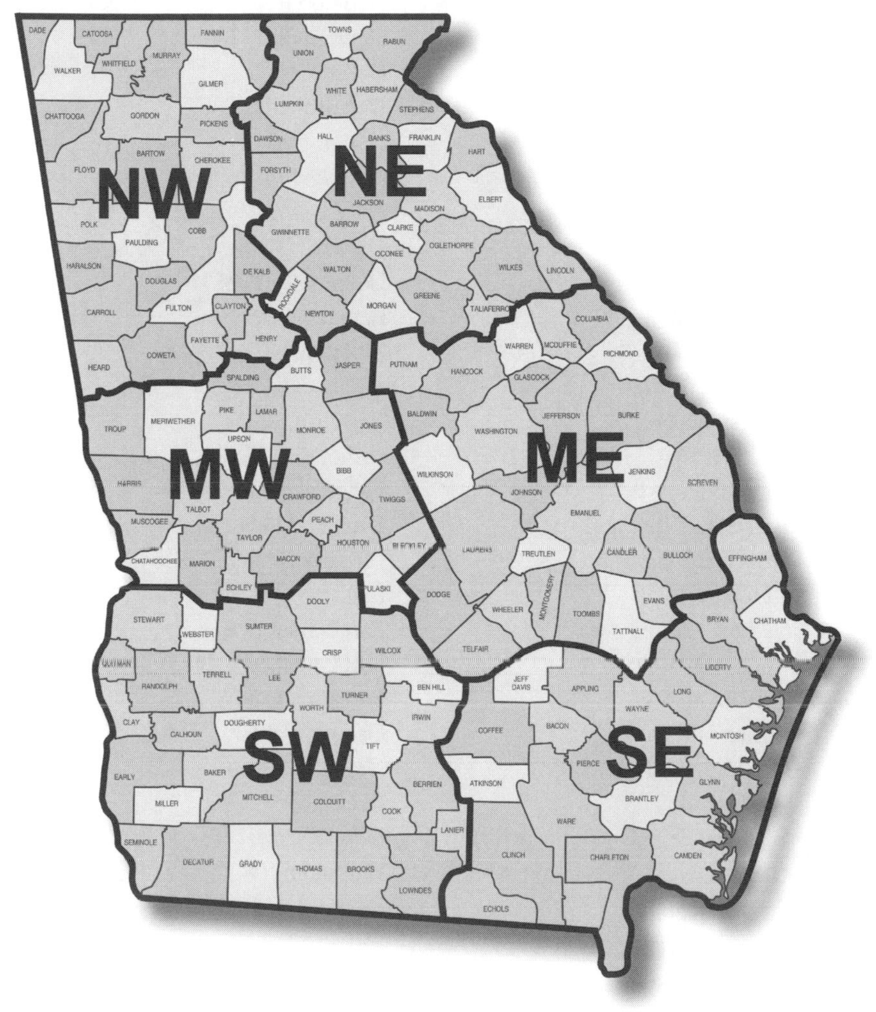

Chapter Area Map

CITY INDEX (Listed by City & Area)

Adairsville, NW
Adel, SW
Albany, SW
Americus, SW
Andersonville, MW
Appling, ME
Ashburn, SW
Athens, NE
Atlanta, NW
Austell, NW
Augusta, ME
Barnesville, MW
Blairsville, NE
Blakely, SW
Blue Ridge, NE
Braselton, NE
Brunswick, SE
Buford, NE
Calhoun, NW
Canton, NW
Carrollton, NW
Cartersville, NW
Cave Spring, NW
Chatsworth, NW
Clarkesville, NE
Clayton, NE
Cleveland, NE
Colquitt, SW
Columbus, MW
Comer, NE
Conyers, NE
Cordele, SW
Covington, NE
Crawfordville, NE
Dahlonega, NE
Dallas, NW
Dalton, NW
Darien, SE
Dawsonville, NE
Decatur, NW
Donalsonville, SW
Douglas, SE
Douglasville, NW
Dublin, ME
Duluth, NW
Dunwoody, NW
Eatonton, ME
Elberton, NE
Ellijay, NW
Fairburn, NE
Fargo, SE
Fitzgerald, SW
Flovilla, MW
Flowery Branch, NE
Folkston, SE
Fort Gaines, SW
Fort Oglethorpe, NW
Fort Valley, MW
Gainesville, NE
Gay, SW
Greensboro, NE
Hamilton, MW
Hampton, NW
Hartwell, NE
Helen, NE
Hiawassee, NE
Homer, NE
Jackson, MW
Jefferson, NE
Jekyll Island, SE
Jewell, ME
Jonesboro, NW
Juliette, MW
Kennesaw, NW

CITY INDEX (Listed by City & Area)

Cities appearing in *italics* occur only in the Seasonal Chapter

Acknowledgements

We are most thankful to be blessed with our parents, Barbara (Darrall) Callahan & George and Catherine Zavatsky who help us every way they can – researching, proofing and babysitting. More importantly, they are great sounding boards and offer unconditional support. A special thanks also to Sharon B. *(Michele's sister)* for her local help in the Atlanta area. We're excited to have nephew Blake as another "kid-tester"! So many places around Georgia remind us of family vacations years ago…

We also want to express our thanks to the many Convention & Visitor Bureaus' staff for providing the attention to detail that helps to complete a project. We felt very welcome during our travels in Georgia and would be proud to call it home!

Our own kids, Jenny and Daniel, were delightful and fun children during our trips across the state. What a joy it is to be their parents…we couldn't do it without them as our "kid-testers"!

We both sincerely thank each other – our partnership has created an even greater business/personal "marriage" with lots of exciting moments, laughs, and new adventures in life woven throughout. Above all, we praise the Lord for His so many blessings through the last few years.

We think Georgia is a wonderful, friendly area of the country with more activities than you could imagine. Our sincere wish is that this book will help everyone "fall in love" with Georgia.

In a Hundred Years…

It will not matter, The size of my bank account…

The kind of house that I lived in, the kind of car that I drove…

But what will matter is…

That the world may be different

Because I was important in the life of a child.

\- *author unknown*

HOW TO USE THIS BOOK

If you are excited about discovering Georgia, this is the book for you and your family! We've spent over a thousand hours doing all the scouting, collecting and compiling (*and most often visiting!*) so that you could spend less time searching and more time having fun.

Here are a few hints to make your adventures run smoothly:

- ❑ Consider the **child's age** before deciding to take a visit.
- ❑ Know **directions** and parking. Call ahead (or visit the company's website) if you have questions *and* bring this book. Also, don't forget your camera! *(please honor rules regarding use).*
- ❑ **Estimate the duration** of the trip. Bring small surprises (favorite juice boxes) travel books, and toys.
- ❑ Call ahead for **reservations** or details, if necessary.
- ❑ Most listings are **closed major holidays** unless noted.
- ❑ Make a **family "treasure chest"**. Decorate a big box or use an old popcorn tin. Store memorabilia from a fun outing, journals, pictures, brochures and souvenirs. Once a year, look through the "treasure chest" and reminisce. "Kids Love Travel Memories!" is an excellent travel journal & scrapbook that your family can create. *(See the order form in back of this book).*
- ❑ Plan **picnics** along the way. Many State History sites and state parks are scattered throughout Georgia. Allow time for a rural /scenic route to take advantage of these free picnic facilities.
- ❑ Some activities, especially tours, require **groups** of 10 or more. To participate, you may either ask to be part of another tour group or get a group together yourself (neighbors, friends, organizations). If you arrange a group outing, most places offer discounts.
- ❑ For the latest **updates** corresponding to the pages in this book, visit our website: **www.KidsLoveTravel.com.**
- ❑ Each chapter represents an area of the state. Each listing is further identified by city, zip code, and place/event name. Our popular **Activity Index** in the back of the book **lists places by Activity Heading** (i.e. State History, Tours, Outdoors, Museums, etc.).

<u>MISSION STATEMENT</u>

At first glance, you may think that this is a book that just lists hundreds of places to travel. While it is true that we've invested thousands of hours of exhaustive research (*and drove over 4000 miles in Georgia*) to prepare this travel resource…just listing places to travel is <u>not</u> the mission statement of these projects.

As children, Michele and I were able to travel extensively throughout the United States. We consider these family times some of the greatest memories we cherish today. We, quite frankly, felt that most children had this opportunity to travel with their family as we did. However, as we became adults and started our own family, we found that this wasn't necessarily the case. We continually heard friends express several concerns when deciding how to spend "quality" and "quantity" family time. 1) What to do? 2) Where to do it? 3) How much will it cost? 4) How do I know that my kids will enjoy it?

Interestingly enough, as we compare our experiences with our families when we were kids, many of our fondest memories were not made at an expensive attraction, but rather when it was least expected.

It is our belief and mission statement that if you as a family will study and <u>use</u> the contained information <u>to create family memories</u>, these memories will grow a stronger, tighter family. Our ultimate mission statement is, that your children will develop a love and a passion for quality family experiences that they can pass to another generation of family travelers.

We thank you for purchasing this book, and we hope to see you on the road (*and hear your travel stories!*) God bless your journeys and happy exploring!

George, Michele, Jenny and Daniel

GENERAL INFORMATION

Call *(or visit the websites)* for the services of interest. Request to be added to their mailing lists.

- Georgia State Parks, (800) 864-7275. **www.gastateparks.org/**
- Georgia Travel Information, (800) VISIT-GA or **www.GeorgiaOnMyMind.org**
- **MW** - Macon-Bibb County Convention & Visitors Bureau (800) 768-3401 or **www.maconga.org**
- **NE** - Augusta Metro Convention & Visitors Bureau - (800) 726-0243 or **www.AugustaGA.org**
- **NE** - Augusta Parks and Rec Department - (706) 796-5025.
- **NE** - Georgia Mountains Regional Tourism - **www.GeorgiaOnMyMind.org**
- **NW** - Atlanta Convention & Visitors Bureau - (800) ATLANTA or **www.atlanta.net**
- **NW** - Cobb County Parks & Recreation - (770) 528-8813
- **SE** - Brunswick and the Golden Isles (St. Simons, Sea Island, Jekyll Island). CVB - (800) 933-COAST or **www.bgivb.com**
- **SE** - Glynn County Recreation and Parks Department (638-2393 or 554-7780)
- **SE** - Savannah Area Convention & Visitors Bureau - **www.savannah-visit.com**

Check out these businesses / services in your area for tour ideas:

AIRPORTS

All children love to visit the airport! Why not take a tour and understand all the jobs it takes to run an airport? Tour the terminal, baggage claim, gates and security / currency exchange. Maybe you'll even get to board a plane.

ANIMAL SHELTERS

Great for the would-be pet owner. Not only will you see many cats and dogs available for adoption, but a guide will show you the clinic and explain the needs of a pet. Be prepared to have the children "fall in love" with one of the animals while they are there!

BANKS

Take a "behind the scenes" look at automated teller machines, bank vaults and drive-thru window chutes. You may want to take this tour and then open a savings account for your child.

CITY HALLS

Halls of Fame, City Council Chambers & Meeting Room, Mayor's Office and famous statues.

ELECTRIC COMPANY / POWER PLANTS

Modern science has created many ways to generate electricity today, but what really goes on with the "flip of a switch". Because coal can be dirty, wear old, comfortable clothes. Coal furnaces heat water, which produces steam, that propels turbines, that drives generators, that make electricity.

FIRE STATIONS

Many Open Houses in October, Fire Prevention Month. Take a look into the life of the firefighters servicing your area and try on their gear. See where they hang out, sleep and eat. Hop aboard a real-life fire engine truck and learn fire safety too.

HOSPITALS

Some Children's Hospitals offer pre-surgery and general tours.

NEWSPAPERS

You'll be amazed at all the new technology. See monster printers and robotics. See samples in the layout department and maybe try to put together your own page. After seeing a newspaper made, most companies give you a free copy (dated that day) as your souvenir. National Newspaper Week is in October.

RESTAURANTS

PIZZA HUT & PAPA JOHN'S

- ❑ Participating locations

Telephone the store manager. Best days are Monday, Tuesday and Wednesday mid-afternoon. Minimum of 10 people. Small charge per person. All children love pizza – especially when they can create their own! As the children tour the kitchen, they learn how to make a pizza, bake it, and then eat it. The admission charge generally includes lots of creatively made pizzas, beverage and coloring book.

KRISPY KREME DONUTS

- ❑ Participating locations

Get an "inside look" and learn the techniques that make these donuts some of our favorites! Watch the dough being made in "giant" mixers, being formed into donuts and taking a "trip" through the fryer. Seeing them being iced and topped with colorful sprinkles is always a favorite with the kids. Contact your local store manager. They prefer Monday or Tuesday. Free.

SUPERMARKETS

Kids are fascinated to go behind the scenes of the same store where Mom and Dad shop. Usually you will see them grind meat, walk into large freezer rooms, watch cakes and bread bake and receive free samples along the way. Maybe you'll even get to pet a live lobster!

TV / RADIO STATIONS

Studios, newsrooms, Fox kids clubs. Why do weathermen never wear blue clothes on TV? What makes a "DJ's" voice sound so deep and smooth?

WATER TREATMENT PLANTS

A giant science experiment! You can watch seven stages of water treatment. The favorite is usually the wall of bright buttons flashing as workers monitor the different processes.

U.S. MAIN POST OFFICES

Did you know Ben Franklin was the first Postmaster General (over 200 years ago)? Most interesting is the high-speed automated mail processing equipment. Learn how to address envelopes so they will be sent quicker (there are secrets). To make your tour more interesting, have your children write a letter to themselves and address it with colorful markers. Mail it earlier that day and they will stay interested trying to locate their letter in all the high-speed machinery.

Chapter 1
Middle East Area - (ME)

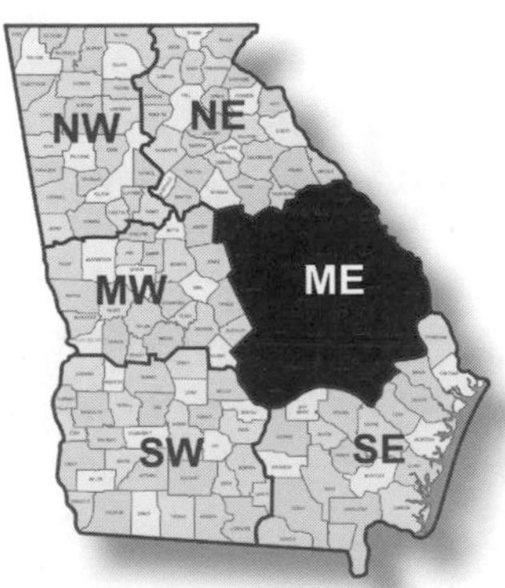

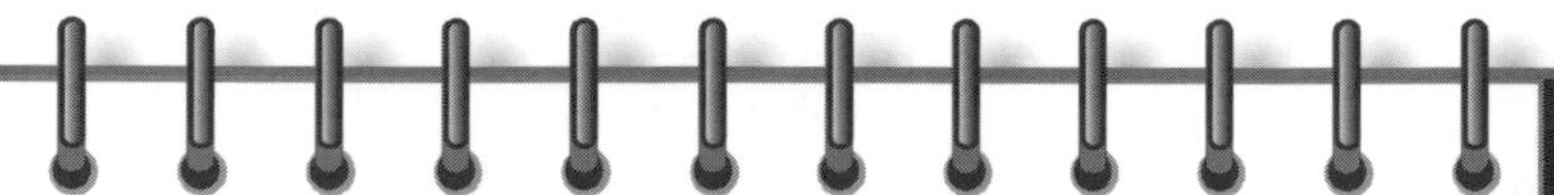

Our Favorites...

* Augusta Canal - Augusta

* Fort Discovery - Augusta

* Woodrow Wilson Boyhood Home - Augusta

* National Forests and State Parks

Ahoy Capt. Daniel - Augusta Canal

MISTLETOE STATE PARK

3723 Mistletoe Road (I-20 exit 175 north 8 miles)

Appling 30802

- Phone: (706) 541-0321, **Web: www.gastateparks.org**
- Hours: Daily 7:00am-10:00pm.
- Admission: FREE. Fee for camping and cottages.

Located on Clarks Hill Lake near Augusta, this park is known as one of the finest bass fishing spots in the nation. Summer guests can cool down at the beach or on miles of shaded nature trails. Canoes and fishing boats may be rented, and a wildlife observation area is available. The park has several fully equipped cottages on the lake, five of which are log cabins. The campground is on a peninsula, offering wonderful views of sunsets over the open water. A multi-camper cabin with electricity and water faces the lake.

AUGUSTA CANAL NATIONAL HERITAGE AREA

1450 Greene Street (3/4 mile from Riverwalk Downtown, Enterprise Mill complex, I-20 exit 200), **Augusta** 30901

- Phone: (706) 823-7089, **Web: www.augustacanal.com**
- Hours: Monday-Saturday 10:00am-6:00pm, Sunday 1:00-6:00pm.
- Admission: Center: $6.00 adult, $5.00 senior (55+) & Military, $4.00 youth (4-18). Boat: Add $2.00 per person. Purchase tickets inside the Interpretive Center.
- Tours: One-hour boat tour: Monday-Friday, 11:30am, 1:30pm, 3:00pm. Saturday departures: 10:00am, 11:30am, 1:30pm. Passengers may bring beverages on board. Winter tours vary.

Augusta Canal National Heritage Area *(cont.)*

- ❑ Miscellaneous: Canoe, walk or bike the historic Canal and its towpath and trails. Pass restored lockkeepers, cottage, dance pavilion and barbeque pit.

Learn the history of the nation's only industrial power canal still in use for its original purposes (the canal is still used for supply water and water power to the city). Visit the interactive Canal Interpretive Center, located in a reclaimed 19th century textile mill where models, machinery, and movies tell the story of the Industrial Revolution in the New South. The Canal was built to control water from the Savannah River for the textile industry in 1845. Exhibits illustrate how waterpower was harnessed, creating electricity to run the factories (try generating power yourself operating a flywheel), provide lighting and the streetcar system. Gaze through the mill floor itself to view the huge mill-race as canal water surges beneath your feet on its way to and from turbines. Hands-on activities such as the "Bobbin game" encourage motor skills and speed as kids must beat the clock to spool bobbins, much like the original mill operation. Handwritten letters and oral histories tell stories of mill families. A walk-in mill house display is complete with furniture demonstrating the living conditions in those days. Lots of "Oh, look at this!" here. The Petersburg Boats were utilized to transport cotton and other goods to and from the mills. You can now ride part of the original canal path. Shallow tour boats take passengers (vs. cargo) along half the length of the canal. Pass old mill factories still in use, historic mill homes, several bridges or overpasses and look for yellow-bellied slider turtles. The kids even get to captain the boat on the way back. Well done, well done!

AUGUSTA MUSEUM OF HISTORY

560 Reynolds Street (between 5th and 6th Street)

Augusta 30901

- Phone: (706) 722-8454, **Web: www.augustamuseum.org**
- Hours: Tuesday-Saturday 10:00am-5:00pm, Sunday 1:00-5:00pm.
- Admission: $4.00 adult, $3.00 senior, $2.00 student (K-12).

This museum's multi-media permanent exhibit, "Augusta's Story", traces 12,000 years of local history from a 10,000 year old projectile point to a 1914 locomotive. The site presents the events, people and forces that shaped the community. Children can participate in hands-on history in the Children's Discovery Gallery. Find out about the important role of local medicine to the community.

BOYHOOD HOME OF PRESIDENT WOODROW WILSON

419 Seventh Street

Augusta 30901

- Phone: (706) 722-9828, **Web: www.historicaugusta.org**
- Hours: Tuesday-Saturday 10:00am-5:00pm.
- Admission: $5.00 adult, $4.00 senior (60+), $3.00 student (K-12).

Thomas Woodrow Wilson was inaugurated as the 28th President of the United States on March 4, 1913. In 1917, during his second term, the United States entered the First World War and Wilson played an international role in the negotiation of the Treaty of Versailles and the organization of the League of Nations. "Tommy" lived in this house for 10 years of his childhood in Augusta. Hear stories of the hardships of the Civil War and Reconstruction, baseball clubs and being raised in a minister's home. Do you think he was a Mamma's Boy? Who put the scuff marks in the dining room table? How do we know Woodrow "borrowed" his mother's diamond ring? (clue: what about the etchings on the window?). You'll see many original furnishings of the Wilson family within the home.

FORT DISCOVERY, NATIONAL SCIENCE CENTERS

One Seventh Street (Riverwatch Pkwy exit 200, left on Riverwatch to downtown, left on 10th St., then right on Reynolds Street)

Augusta 30901

- Phone: (706) 821-0200 or (800) 325-5445
  Web: www.nationalsciencecenter.org
- Hours: Monday-Saturday 10:00am-5:00pm, Sunday Noon-5:00pm. Closed New Years, Easter, Thanksgiving, & Xmas.
- Admission: $8.00 adult, $6.00 senior, active military, child. Discovery Theater and StarLab Planetarium $2.00 extra.
- Miscellaneous: The museum faces Augusta's Riverwalk, the landscaped scene of passing boaters, bikers, walkers and such. Beautiful views and areas for gathering.

Fort Discovery is an educational haven for kids of all ages. The two-story interactive site is complete with more than 270 math, science and technology exhibits. Exhibits range from indoor lightning to pendulum swings, "chopping up" sound into bits and thermal imaging technology. Slide around and down the two-story Martian Tower or witness Morse code via a water fountain, super soaker display. Play virtual sports, ride a motorcycle or a magnetic car - all using principles of math and motion to operate. Then, try the Dual Robot Arm and its fingers. Outside ride the high-wire bicycle and a medical helicopter that transmits your vital signs to an aid station inside the center. Recommended for all age children, first floor for younger, second for older. Lots of modern, high tech science we haven't "played with" before.

PHINIZY SWAMP NATURE PARK

1858 Lock & Dam Road (Lock & Dam Road, near the airport)

Augusta 30901

- Phone: (706) 828-2109, **Web: www.phinizyswamp.org**
- Hours: Open dawn to dusk.

Visitors can enjoy the natural resources of the swamp and its wildlands at this 1150-acre urban nature park via trails, boardwalks, observation decks. A newer boardwalk enables visitors to "walk across the swamp". Look for blue heron, otters and alligators.

OCONEE NATIONAL FOREST

1199 Madison Road, **Eatonton** 31024

- Phone: (706) 485-7110

Many visitors enjoy Oconee's recreation facilities - daily, for FREE. There are camping areas; trails for horses, hikers, and all-terrain vehicles; boat launches, picnic areas; and wildlife viewing areas. Annually, the Oconee hosts a Kid's Fishing Rodeo to promote outdoor activities for young people. Come and visit some of the more popular sites, such as Skull Shoals Historic Area, Dyar Pasture waterfowl habitat, Falling Creek beaver pond, and the newly restored Miller Lake.

LITTLE OCMULGEE STATE PARK & LODGE

P O Drawer 149 (2 miles north of town via US 319 and 441)

McRae 31055

- Phone: (229) 868-6651, **Web: www.gastateparks.org**
- Hours: Daily 7:00am-10:00pm. Lodge hours 6:00am-midnight.
- Admission: FREE. Fee for camping, cottages and lodge overnights.

Little Ocmulgee State Park & Lodge *(cont.)*

Boaters and anglers will enjoy the park's 265-acre lake that includes a swimming beach. Hikers enjoy the Oak Ridge Trail winding through scrub oaks and pines towards a buzzard roost and boardwalk (2.5 mile trail). The renovated lodge offers hotel-style guest rooms, a restaurant with golf course view, and a swimming pool and tennis courts. There are campsite, cottage and canoe/pedal boat rentals and a mini-golf course within the park, too.

FORT MORRIS STATE HISTORIC SITE

2559 Fort Morris Road (I-95 exit 76 via Islands Highway and Fort Morris Road)

Midway 31320

- Phone: (912) 884-5999, **Web: www.gastateparks.org**
- Hours: Tuesday-Saturday 9:00am-5:00pm, Sunday 2:00-5:30pm. Closed Mondays (except holidays).
- Admission: $1.50-$2.50.

When the Continental Congress convened in 1776, the delegates recognized the importance of a fort to protect their growing seaport from the British. When the British demanded the fort's surrender in 1778, the defiant Col. John McIntosh replied, "Come and take it!" The British refused and withdrew back to Florida. This Revolutionary War fort was eventually captured by the British in 1779, then used again by Americans during the war of 1812. Today, visitors can stand within the earthwork remains and view scenic Saint Catherine's Sound. A museum and film describe the colonial port of Sunbury and the site's history. There is a one mile nature trail on the premises.

SEABROOK VILLAGE

660 Trade Hill Road (east on US 84, four miles east of I-95, turn left on Trade Hill Road)

Midway 31320

- Phone: (912) 884-7008, **Web: www.libertytrail.com/seabrook.html**
- Hours: Tuesday-Saturday 10:00am-5:00pm and by special arrangement.
- Admission: $1.50-$2.50 for walking tours. Fees vary for groups.
- Tours: Interactive tours available for groups of 15 or more.
- Miscellaneous: Special events include story-telling, hay rides, cane grinding, clay chimney building, Country Christmas and more.

Seabrook Village features eight turn-of-the-century buildings on a developing 104-acre site. Visit the one-room Seabrook School where "reading and writing and arithmetic were taught to the tune of a hick'ry stick." Next, visit the homesteads and try your hand at grinding corn into meal and grits or washing clothes on a scrub board. Exhibits include the Material Culture Collection of hand-made items from a peanut roaster to twig furniture. Planned group visits (our recommendation to get the full effect) are fully interactive as costumed interpreters engage visitors in all aspects of old time village life.

MAGNOLIA SPRINGS STATE PARK

1053 Magnolia Springs Drive (5 miles north of Millen on US 25)

Millen 30442

- Phone: (478) 982-1660, **Web: www.gastateparks.org**
- Hours: Daily 7:00am-10:00pm. Aquarium: Daily 9:00am-4:00pm.
- Admission: FREE. Fee for camping and cottages.

Magnolia Springs State Park *(cont.)*

The park is known for its crystal clear springs flowing 7 million gallons of water per day and the beautiful boardwalk which spans the cool water. Visitors may watch for alligators, turtles and other wildlife near the springs. A free, freshwater aquarium features native species to the area. The 28-acre lake is available for fishing and boating. Historically, during the Civil War, the site was called Camp Lawton and served as "the world's largest prison." Today, little remains of the prison stockade except some earthen breastworks. Hikers and bikers can enjoy the 10 miles of trails.

HAMBURG STATE PARK

6071 Hamburg State Park Road (off GA 102, 20 miles north of Sandersville)

Mitchell 30820

- Phone: (478) 552-2393, **Web: www.gastateparks.org**
- Hours: Daily 7:00am-10:00pm.
- Admission: FREE. Camping fee.

Hamburg State Park offers a wonderful mix of history and outdoor recreation. Anglers can enjoy great lake fishing for largemouth bass, crappie and bream, as well as boat ramps and a fishing pier. Campers find shaded campsites along the edge of the lake. The restored 1921 water-powered grist mill is still operational and beckons visitors to buy a bag of corn meal at the country store (call ahead to ask when it will be operating). The mill museum displays old agricultural tools and appliances used in rural Georgia.

GORDONIA-ALATAMAHA STATE PARK

P O Box 1039 (just off US 280, I-16 exit 98)

Reidsville 30453

- Phone: (912) 557-7744, **Web: www.gastateparks.org**
- Hours: Daily 7:00am-10:00pm.
- Admission: FREE. Fee for camping and golf.

Gordonia-Alatamaha's unusual name comes from the rare Gordonia tree - a member of the bay family - and the original spelling of the nearby Altamaha River. This park is a favorite for picnicking, family reunions and golf. Picnic tables and shelters surround a small lake, where visitors can swim or rent pedal boats and fishing boats during warmer months (no private boats allowed). Docks are available for anglers and children enjoy looking for beaver dams from the observation deck.

SPARTA-HANCOCK MUSEUM

325 Broad Street (downtown)

Sparta 31087

- Phone: (706) 444-7462
  Web: www.historicspartahancock.org/museum.htm
- Hours: Monday-Friday 9:00am-5:00pm.
- Admission: $1.00-$3.00 (age 6+).

The county museum collection is known for its display of handmade quilts and African-American carved items. See the exhibit on the life of famous Hancock County resident Amanda America Dickson, whose life was portrayed in Showtime's original film "A House Divided" (starring Jennifer Beals). A true story of a 19th Century wealthy plantation owner's daughter who discovers the truth about her race percentage.

OGEECHEE GRIST MILL

Union Church Road, **Sparta (Jewell)** 31045

- Phone: (706) 465-9683
- Admission: FREE
- Tours: Mondays & Wednesdays at 8:30am. Call in advance for confirmation.

Not many things are done as they were 150-200 years ago but Alvester "cabbage" Allen grinds corn meal just like they did centuries ago. See how good, old-fashioned ground Georgia corn meal is milled. He starts by lifting the gates impounding the Ogeechee River, allowing tons of water to flow through the turbine. A wheel in the mill house is turned, activating a shaft and the mill rumbles into action. The millstones are made of a special kind of granite. One stone is about 6" thick and is stationary. The other, is two tons, and is rotated by waterpower. As the cracked corn is slowly fed into the hole, out below comes a small stream of fine corn meal, which is warm when it comes from the stones. You'll love the smell! Try the "Ogeechee Hush Puppy Mix".

GEORGIA SOUTHERN UNIVERSITY NATURE CENTERS

(GA 25 to US 301, North Mail Street. Follow signs)

Statesboro 30460

- **Web: www.georgiasouthern.edu/public.php**
- Admission: FREE

The University has three great areas for family learning and adventure:

- CENTER FOR WILDLIFE EDUCATION AND THE RAPTOR CENTER - Five acres in the heart of campus provide a center including a self-guided nature walk through six habitat displays, housing eleven species of live birds of prey. Within these habitats, wetlands, mountains, and forest you have an opportunity to view native raptors in their natural environments. An elevated walkway allows visitors an unobstructed and up-close encounter with a Bald Eagle nest, complete with a live Eagle! The Children's Discovery Trail has 17 exploratory stations and an eagle nest "fly-in" area. The Pavilion or Amphitheater hold flighted raptor demonstrations (rain or shine). Falconers fly several species of birds of prey while explaining the various adaptations the wounded birds must make. Take the field guide challenge indoors through the Center's hands-on encounter displays. Try to locate and identify the 50+ animals inhabiting the exhibit. Also indoors, you will find the reptile program including hands-on reptiles and amphibians. (912-681-0831, Weekdays 9:00am-5:00pm, Weekends 1:00-5:00pm. Public demos on weekends. Group tours, weekdays. Closed summer Sundays.)

- ❑ BOTANICAL GARDENS - The native Southern and coastal gardens surround an old cottage. Volunteer for the Children's Vegetable Garden where you'll learn to cultivate the soil, nurture seeds and finally harvest vegetables. Each Wednesday, you'll work in the garden with staff and volunteers to grow produce to donate to the Statesboro Food Bank. (1505 Bland Avenue. 912-871-1149, open 9:00am-dusk. Tours by appointment.)
- ❑ MUSEUM - Traveling natural history displays might have you reconstruct ancient structures or dig for dino eggs. A 25-foot fossil of a prehistoric Mosasaur greets visitors along with the oldest whale fossil found in North America. (Southern Drive, Rosenwald Bldg., 912-681-5444. Weekdays 9:00am-5:00pm, weekends 2:00-5:00pm.)

GEORGE L. SMITH STATE PARK

371 George L. Smith State Park Road (I-16 exit 104, off GA 23)

Twin City 30471

- Phone: (478) 763-2759, **Web: www.gastateparks.org**
- Hours: Daily 7:00am-10:00pm.
- Admission: FREE. Fee for camping and cottages.

The park is named after one of Georgia's great legislators. With lakeside camping and cozy cottages, this secluded park is the perfect south Georgia retreat. It is best known for the Parrish Mill, a combination grist mill, sawmill, covered bridge and dam built in 1880 and still open for tours. Anglers and canoeists can explore the mill pond dotted with Spanish moss-draped trees and home to blue heron and gopher tortoises. There are 11 miles of walking and biking trails.

VIDALIA ONION FACTORY

US Hwy 280E (I-16 south to US 1 east to Lyons. Turn right on Hwy 280, straight about 3 miles)

Vidalia 30474

- Phone: (912) 526-3466, **Web: www.vidaliaonion.com**
- Tours: Pre-arranged through Vidalia Area CVB at (912) 538-8687.
- Miscellaneous: A small sandwich shop is within the store.

Do you love Vidalia Onions? A visit to the Vidalia Onion Factory is a perfect way to make your trip yummy (free samples) and fun (interesting onion facts). You'll see it on the left side of the highway - in the middle of an onion field! The Vidalia sweet onion was first grown back in 1931. It is a family business, owned and operated by Stanley Farms. Several hundred acres are devoted to Georgia's Official State Vegetable - the sweet Vidalia Onion. Farmers and scientists have concluded that the loamy soil and mild temperatures combine to give the Vidalia Onion its sweet taste. In fact, the Vidalia Onion can only be grown in 14 southeast Georgia counties and parts of six others. Free seasonal factory tours are available with advanced scheduling. Harvesting and processing begins in mid-April and continues through mid-June.

SUGGESTED LODGING AND DINING

COUNTRY SUITES AUGUSTA RIVERWALK – **Augusta**. 3 Ninth Street, **www.countryinns.com/augustaga_riverwalk**. (I-20 exit 200 Riverwatch Pkwy, left on 10th, right on Reynolds). (706) 774-1400. Family-friendly amenities in the middle of the heart of downtown Augusta. Complimentary light and healthy breakfast, in-room coffee, frig and microwave; lending book library; wireless internet access; and indoor pool. Best of all, spacious, one-bedroom suites with room for everyone.

Chapter 2
Middle West Area - (MW)

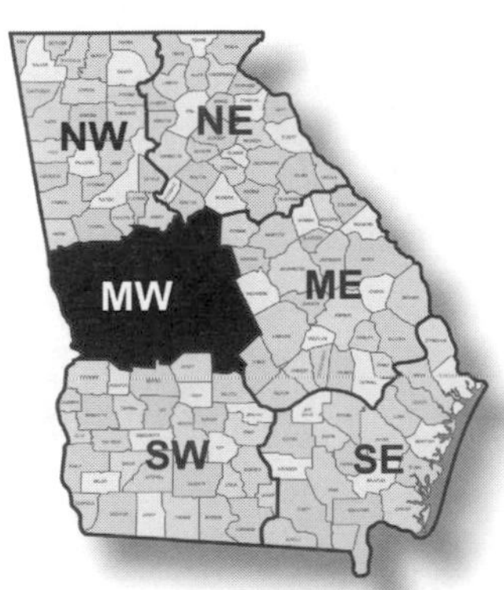

Our Favorites...

* Port Columbus - Columbus

* Blue Bird Bus Company - Fort Valley

* Lane Peach Packing Company - Fort Valley

* Whistle Stop Cafe - Juliette

* Georgia Music Hall of Fame - Macon

* Georgia Sports Hall of Fame - Macon

* Ocmulgee Indian Mounds - Macon

"The Thrill of Victory"
- Georgia Sports Hall of Fame

ANDERSONVILLE NATIONAL HISTORIC SITE/ NATIONAL POW MUSEUM

496 Cemetery Rd (I-75 exit Hwy 26 or 27 heading west, follow signs)

Andersonville 31711

- Phone: (229) 924-0343, **Web: www.nps.gov/ande/**
- Hours: Daily 8:30am-5:00pm
- Admission: FREE
- Tours: Walking and/or driving through the National Cemetery and prison site are recommended. An audio driving tour is available for a $1.00 rental fee.
- Miscellaneous: A picnic area is located within the park. Interpretive Programs are presented at the historic prison site daily at 11:00am and 2:00pm. Nearby is DRUMMER BOY CIVIL WAR MUSEUM, a small museum with full uniform displays and a large diorama depicting Andersonville confederate Prison and the village in 1864 (114 Church St, 229-924-2558, open Thursday-Sunday afternoons).

Andersonville, or Camp Sumter as it was officially known, was one of the largest of many Confederate military prisons established during the Civil War. During the 14 months the prison existed, more than 45,000 Union soldiers were confined here. Of these, almost 13,000 died from disease, poor sanitation, malnutrition, overcrowding, or exposure to the elements. The only park in the National Park System to serve as a memorial to all American prisoners of war throughout the nation's history, this 515 acre park consists of the original historic prison site complete with rebuilt stockade wall sections and remnants of escape tunnels, as well as the National Cemetery and the Civil War cemetery. A 27-minute audio-visual program entitled "Echoes of Captivity" provides an orientation to the overall prisoner of war story. We would suggest families participate in the Prison Historical Hike - a 3-mile walking historic hike designed to acquaint young hikers with the story of Andersonville and American prisoners of war. The hike is not along a physical trail, but allows an exploration of the park through the use of a questionnaire to direct your visit.

COCA-COLA SPACE SCIENCE CENTER

701 Front Avenue (Columbus State University), **Columbus** 31901

- ❑ Phone: (706) 649-1470, **Web: www.ccssc.org**
- ❑ Hours: Monday-Thursday 10:00am-4:00pm, Friday 10:00am-8:00pm, Saturday 10:30am-8:00pm. Closed Mondays in winter.
- ❑ Admission: Admission to the Center is free. Admission is charged for planetarium shows ($3.00-$4.00) and Challenger Learning Center missions.

The Exhibit Hall includes: Space Suit and Apollo Capsule replicas. The Telescopes Exhibit looks at various large telescopes located around the world and displays some of the images taken with them. The Coca-Cola drink dispenser is a replica of the first such beverage machine taken into space. The Space Shuttle Orbiter is a full size replica of the first 50 feet of the NASA space shuttle orbiter. Inside there is a mini theater, comprising of 26 seats and a video screen. The Orbiter is used as part of our Challenger Learning Center to launch the students into space and from there, they proceed through an air lock into the Space Station. Groups of 20-30 can experience a simulated mission in the Challenger Learning Center on an appointment basis. The Mead Observatory is open to the public once a month for astronomical viewing.

COLUMBUS SYMPHONY ORCHESTRA

900 Broadway (RiverCenter for the Performing Arts, downtown)

Columbus 31901

- Phone: (706) 323-5059 or (888) 332-5200, **Web: www.csoga.org**

Founded in 1855 by Mendelssohn's student, Herman S. Saroni, the Columbus Symphony Orchestra became the third orchestra formed in the United States. The symphony disbanded during the Civil War and both World Wars, but always reorganized during times of peace. In 1949, the organization as we know it today, was formed and has performed for 51 consecutive years. Kids under eight will most enjoy CSO Family Concerts. Activities include an instrument petting zoo; a chance to meet the musicians and hear them play close-up; musical games (complete with prizes); and a special concert including musical stories.

OXBOW MEADOWS ENVIRONMENTAL LEARNING CENTER

3535 S. Lumpkin Road (I-185; take exit 1B, traveling north on Victory Drive (U.S. Hwy 27/280). Drive approx. 2.3 miles to South Lumpkin Road), **Columbus** 31901

- Phone: (706) 687-4090, **Web: www.oxbow.colstate.edu**
- Hours: Tuesday-Saturday 10:00am-5:00pm, Sunday Noon-5:00pm.
- Admission: FREE

The Environmental Learning Center is a hands-on interpretative facility focusing on the natural history of the region. Displays include mounted specimens of mammals, birds, reptiles, and a small live animal collection of regional reptiles, insects, amphibians, and fish. Two walking trails wind between ponds taking hikers around native flora and fauna. There is a new treetop walkway - the first phase in a system of suspended canopy trails that will allow visitors to literally walk among the treetops! Walk along suspended bridges and stop at a viewing platform designed for observation. For the nature lover, butterflies, birds, turtles, and dragonflies can be found in abundance.

PORT COLUMBUS NATIONAL CIVIL WAR NAVAL MUSEUM

1002 Victory Drive (off Rte. 27/280, downtown. South Commons near the Civic Center), **Columbus** 31901

- Phone: (706) 327-9798, **Web: www.portcolumbus.org**
- Hours: Daily 9:00am-5:00pm. Closed Christmas Day.
- Admission: $3.00-$4.50 (age 7+).

Columbus, Georgia was the site of a Confederate Naval Shipyard. The largest product of this facility was the CSS Jackson, one of the largest of the ironclads built in the south. The Jackson was nearly 225 feet long, 54 feet wide and weighed 2000 tons. The Jackson's remains are displayed in an elevated form. This 40,000 square foot facility also features the remains of two original Civil War Confederate Navy ships and full-size sectional reconstructions of the U.S.S. Monitor. Look at vessels, uniforms, equipment and weapons used by the Union and Confederate navies. Interactive exhibits, including a Confederate ironclad ship simulator, offer the visitor an opportunity to experience 19th century naval combat first hand.

COLUMBUS MUSEUM

1251 Wynnton Road (off 10th Avenue, outskirts of downtown)

Columbus 31906

- Phone: (706) 649-0713, **Web: www.columbusmuseum.com**
- Hours: Tuesday-Saturday 10:00am-5:00pm, Thursdays until 9:00pm, Sunday 1:00-5:00pm. Closed legal holidays.
- Admission: FREE

The second-largest art museum in Georgia and one of the largest in the Southeast, the Columbus Museum is particularly known for its concentration on American art and the history of the Chattahoochee River Valley. In addition to its 15 permanent collection and traveling exhibition galleries of fine and decorative art, the Museum offers visitors the chance to investigate color and texture in Transformations, a hands-on discovery gallery. In this area, kids can create patterns on a magnet board, mix colors on a light table, explore basic shapes in a building block room, and step into works from their permanent collection. Visitors also can trace the development of the Chattahoochee Valley area in Chattahoochee Legacy, a regional history gallery displaying artifacts with its own award-winning film (shown several times daily).

INDIAN SPRINGS STATE PARK

678 Lake Clark Road (I-75 southbound, exit 205 to Jackson, south on GA 42 to the park)

Flovilla 30216

- Phone: (770) 504-2277, **Web: www.gastateparks.org**
- Hours: Daily 7:00am-10:00pm
- Admission: FREE. Fee for camping and cottages.

Indian Springs is thought to be the oldest state park in the United States. The area was once home to Creek Indians who used the springs for centuries to heal the sick and impart extra vigor to anyone. Then, the area became a bustling resort town. Today, visitors can still sample the spring water while enjoying the park's cottages, camping, swimming, boating and fishing. Many structures were built during the Great Depression by FDR's Civilian Conservation Corps. A museum highlights the original inhabitants, the Creeks, the resort era and the CCC building projects. There is also a 3/4 mile nature trail and a miniature golf course within the park.

BLUE BIRD BUS COMPANY

402 Blue Bird Blvd.

Fort Valley 31030

- Phone: (478) 822-2546 or (800) 486-7122
  Web: www.blue-bird.com
- Hours: Monday-Thursday 7:30am-5:00pm, Friday 8:00am-Noon.
- Admission: FREE
- Tours: Tour the school bus division by appointment only. Tours of the Wanderlodge motor home makers are offered Monday-Thursday 10:00am and 2:00pm.

Blue Bird Corporation is one of the world's leading bus manufacturers, delivering thousands of school buses, commercial buses and recreational vehicles to the market each year. Over 75 years ago, a friend of Albert L. Luce, Sr., the founder of Blue Bird, asked for a bus to transport his workers. This request gave Luce the opportunity to create the first Blue Bird school bus and spearheaded the beginning of a highly successful corporation. On tour, you watch as the workers surround a bus like bees. Why is it good to see a row of green lights? How do they run buses for 5 miles without moving? You'll see the "guts" of the same type of school bus you may ride in - you'll even see its "ribs". You have no idea how a giant vehicle like this is hand-made until you visit.

LANE PEACH PACKING COMPANY

50 Lane Road (I-75 exit 142 west on Hwy 96. Look for the rows and rows of crop trees -you can't miss it)

Fort Valley 31030

- Phone: (478) 825-3592 or (800) 277-3224
  Web: www.lanepacking.com
- Hours: Daily 9:00am-5:00pm. Until dark during Peach season.

- Admission: FREE. $3.00-$5.00 for orchard tours or field trips.
- Tours: Individuals can take the self-guided tour at anytime during the day. Viewing the entire process should take about 30 min. There is no charge for the tours. Due to the nature of the peach crop, they cannot guarantee the packing line will run every day. Guided tours are reserved. Packing line tour available (mid-May – mid-August).
- Miscellaneous: Roadside Market which includes the Peachtree Café and Just Peachy Gift Shop.

This fun and educational attraction grows and ships Georgia peaches and pecans. Lane Packing Company farms over 2,500 acres of peach trees and 2000 acres of pecans. Currently, they grow over 30 varieties of peaches. Begin your visit by watching the farm video in the market. How do they make new peach varieties? In the summer, take a self-guided tour of the packing operation from an elevated platform. Informational signs describe each step of the process. See the peaches line up like soldiers to get their baths! It's different and fun to watch. ORCHARD TOUR - Summer or Fall. Ride tour through the peach and pecan orchards. Tour guides will explain the history of the peach industry in Georgia as well as how these crops are grown and harvested. Call in advance for group reservations. STRAWBERRY FIELD TRIP - Springtime. Young students will enjoy this package tour. Tour guides will explain how strawberries are grown. Each student will pick one pound of berries and will enjoy a cup of fresh strawberry ice cream. A strawberry coloring book will be sent home with each child.

HIGH FALLS STATE PARK

76 High Falls Park Drive (nearly 2 miles east of I-75 exit 198)

Jackson 30233

- Phone: (478) 993-3053, **Web: www.gastateparks.org**
- Hours: Daily 7:00am-10:00pm.
- Admission: FREE. Fee for camping.

This site was a prosperous industrial town with several stores, a cotton gin, a grist mill, blacksmith shop and hotel. Even a shoe factory was in town until a major railroad bypassed it and it became a ghost town in the 1880s. You can enjoy the scenic waterfall or hike to the remaining grist mill foundation. A campground, swimming pool and canoe rental are also available.

JARRELL PLANTATION STATE HISTORIC SITE

Route 2, Box 220 (I75 exit 185 or 171, follow signs)

Juliette 31046

- Phone: (912) 986-5172, **Web: www.gastateparks.org**
- Hours: Tuesday-Saturday 9:00am-5:00pm, Sunday 2:00-5:30pm. Closed Monday except legal holidays, then closed Tuesday of that week.
- Admission: $2.00-$3.50 per person.
- Miscellaneous: Watch the intro video to get an overview.

This middle Georgia plantation consists of 20 buildings dating between 1847 and 1945. The cotton plantation was owned by a single family for more than 140 years. It survived General Sherman's "March to the Sea", typhoid fever, Emancipation, Reconstruction, the cotton boll weevil, the advent of steam power and a transition from farming to forestry. His success might be credited to the many trades produced here by several generations - especially "ginning" and "milling". Among the buildings, machines and tools once used by the Jarrells are a three-story barn, smokehouses, wheat houses, a cane press, cotton gin, grist mill, saw mill, syrup mill, etc. Visitors can tour the 1847 plantation house, carpenter shop, blacksmith shop and other buildings. Inside the 1847 house, you'll see original furnishings, including a baby cradle and a cobbler's bench, many of which were built by family members. During seasonal programs, spinning, weaving, woodstove cooking, blacksmithing and other skills are demonstrated (best time to interactively visit). Kids like seeing crops growing and visiting with the mule.

WHISTLE STOP CAFÉ - FRIED GREEN TOMATOES

443 McCracken Street (I-75 exit 186 east 9 miles)

Juliette 31046

- Phone: (478) 994-3670, **www.thewhistlestopcafe.com**
- Hours: Tuesday-Sunday 11:00am-6:00pm. Tuesday – Sunday 11:00am-4:00pm (winter).

In the early 1900s, Juliette was a booming community along the railroad tracks and the Ocmulgee River. As time went on the economy left Juliette a ghost town. Then, in 1991, the town was re-discovered by the producers of the movie "Fried Green Tomatoes". The quaint buildings and the railroad provided just the right ingredients for the movie. Visitors from all over the country now come to taste those famous fried green tomatoes at the real-life café and enjoy walking down the streets of this very small town. After you dine on original tomatoes and southern food, take a walk and look for the burial site of “Buddy's arm” or the Juliette “Little Opry”. Cute town…and the trains come through faithfully at noon.

AROUND TOWN TOURS - MACON

200 Cherry Street (trolley leaves from Welcome Center, Terminal Station. I-16, exiting and turning onto M.L. King, Jr. Blvd.)

Macon 31201

- Phone: (800) 768-3401, **Web: www.visitmacon.org**
- Hours: Monday-Saturday 9:00am-5:00pm.
- Admission: $15.00 adult, $9.00 youth. Set your own pace and save up to 25% by purchasing their packages.
- Miscellaneous: Tickets are available at the Downtown Visitor Center located in the Terminal Station where you'll find free all day parking.

Around Town Tours offer friendly, local trolley operators who kindly answer questions and give you quick tidbits and access to historical sites around town. You won't need driving directions when you take this tour. It features free trolley transportation & admission into the following attractions:

- CANNONBALL HOUSE - see the still unexploded shell that crashed through the parlor wall and rolled across the floor during an 1864 Federal attack.
- HAY HOUSE - Palace of the South.
- SIDNEY LANIER COTTAGE - see separate listing.

GEORGIA MUSIC HALL OF FAME

200 MLK Jr. Blvd. (I75 to I-16 east to exit 2, near historic Terminal Station, downtown), **Macon** 31201

- Phone: (478) 750-8555, **Web: www.gamusichall.com**
- Hours: Monday-Saturday 9:00am-5:00pm, Sunday 1:00-5:00pm.
- Admission: $8.00 adult, $6.00 senior and student w/ID, $3.50 child (4-16).

Experience the best of Georgia Music from Gospel to Classical. The huge facility features exhibits that include music, video, memorabilia, instruments, performance costumes and more. Walk around the "town" visiting with inductees while listening to the voices of Ray Charles, Otis Redding, Gladys Knight & the Pips, James Brown, and Little Richard, and hundreds more that call (ed) Georgia home. Scream for your favorite videos in the Theater (applause meter selection), share a smile and a tear during the short film in the Gospel Chapel, then cut loose in the nation's only dedicated kids music museum - The Music Factory. The activities in the Music Factory introduce children to various aspects of music and sparks their interest in musical instruments and career possibilities. The children can watch themselves on a big screen TV as they dance to the sounds of Georgia music. Or, travel to the far reaches of the globe as they listen to bits of music from countries far and near. Next, the children can play a piano, violin, guitar, drum, xylophone, tambourine, or guitar. Children can listen to a simple song like "Twinkle, Twinkle Little Star" in the traditional way or as a jazz, salsa or rock tune. Kids can even "make music" as they "slide" down a musical note!

GEORGIA SPORTS HALL OF FAME

301 Cherry Street (I-75 to exit I-16 east to MLK, Jr. exit Cherry St)

Macon 31201

- Phone: (912) 752-1585, **Web: www.gshf.org**
- Hours: Monday-Saturday 9:00am-5:00pm, Sunday 1:00-5:00pm.
- Admission: $8.00 adult, $6.00 senior (60+), Military, College Students; $3.50 child (6-16); $15.00 family.

Begin your sports experience in the museum's theater with a high energy, high emotion film about Georgia sports legends. Next, it's on to the actual exhibit hall, which takes you through sports from prep to professional, including collegiate, amateur, and Olympic achievements. Along the way, you'll have the chance to shoot hoops, kick field goals, throw passes, slam a jump ball, drive a NASCAR simulator and use specially themed computers to see how academics like geography, math and history are critical to athletes and many careers in sports from playing to sports casting to managing. There's even an area to be a media announcer and make your own calls on famous ball plays! That was our favorite part - how excited can you sound?

SIDNEY LANIER COTTAGE

935 High Street (downtown)

Macon 31201

- Phone: (478) 743-3851
  Web: www.cityofmacon.net/Living/slcottage.htm
- Hours: Monday-Friday 9:00am-4:00pm. Last tour begins at 3:30pm. Saturday 9:30am-12:30pm.
- Admission: $3.00-$5.00 per person.

Step back in time with a guided tour of this 1840 cottage that is the birthplace of Sidney Lanier, famous poet and musician of the Old South. He served in the Confederate Army until captured aboard a blockade runner and confined at Fort Lookout, Maryland. Kids' group tours explore 1800s toys and the influences of nature on Lanier's music and poetry. At an early age, Sidney learned to play the flute, violin and many other instruments that imitate sounds in nature (ex. Birds). The museum displays Lanier memorabilia and the gift shop sells books on the Civil War, items on Lanier, and other related articles. Kids with an interest in The Arts are best influenced by sites like this.

TUBMAN AFRICAN AMERICAN MUSEUM

340 Walnut Street (I-75 exit to I-16 east to exit 2, MLK, Jr. Blvd. And turn right. Turn right on Walnut)

Macon 31201

- Phone: (478) 743-8544, **Web: www.tubmanmuseum.com**
- Hours: Monday-Saturday 9:00am-5:00pm, Sunday 2:00-5:00pm.
- Admission: $5.00 adult, $3.00 child (age 4+) and student.

Along the trolley tour, the Tubman is a wonderful experience to learn about African American art, history and culture. Your visit starts with a 63-foot long mural that documents history from ancient Africa to today's leaders and heroes. Kid-friendly exhibits include an inventor's gallery and a fun musical instrument area. A new museum, many times the size, is opening in the near future.

MUSEUM OF ARTS AND SCIENCES

4182 Forsyth Road

Macon 31210

- Phone: (478) 477-3232, **Web: www.masmacon.com**
- Hours: Monday-Saturday 9:00am-5:00pm, Sunday 1:00-5:00pm, Friday open till 9:00pm.
- Admission: $4.00-$7.00.

The museum features changing and permanent exhibits like the 3-story interactive Discovery House, a live animal complex featuring daily live animal shows, daily planetarium shows, an observatory, and nature trails. Examine the beauty of original works of art in an artist's garret, peek into a scientist's workshop and then journey into space.

OCMULGEE NATIONAL MONUMENT INDIAN MOUNDS

1207 Emery Highway (I-75 exit on I-16 east to eastern edge of Macon on US 80 east)

Macon 31217

- Phone: (478) 752-8257, **Web: www.nps.gov/ocmu**
- Hours: Daily 9:00am-5:00pm. Closed Christmas & New Years only
- Admission: FREE
- Miscellaneous: THE OCMULGEE HERITAGE TRAIL is near here. Interstate16 East and then exit 2 at Martin Luther King Blvd. The main access point to the Ocmulgee Heritage Trail, the Spring Street (Interstate 16, exit 1A) entrance provides ample parking and the only boat access to the river along the trail. Gateway Park is at the southern end of the trail, at the Martin Luther King Jr. Bridge (Interstate 16, exit 2) on the South side of the river. It features a spectacular overlook with steps down to the water, an interactive fountain, and a 7-foot bronze statue of late soul singer and Macon native, Otis Redding. Street parking is available.

Between AD 900 and 1100 a skillful forming people lived on this site. They were known as Mississippians - a sedentary people who lived mainly by farming bottomlands for crops of corn, beans, squash, pumpkins, and tobacco. They built a compact town of thatched huts on the bluff overlooking the river. The visitor center houses a museum of items found on site and shows a short film "People of the Macon Plateau" (shown every 30 minutes). Among the artifacts found in the Funeral Mound were a pair of copper sun disks and a copper covered puma jaw, part of a head-dress. Survey the landscape from atop ancient Indian Mounds, listen to tales of the past inside a 1,000 year old ceremonial earth-lodge, hike along nature trails and study archeological remains. Why did they build trenches? What is different about their arrowheads (vs. northern Woodlands)? Our favorite part? - the earthen lodge and oral program inside. What happens to the lodge twice a year (once on Michele's birthday)? Would you be comfortable in their "seats"? This is an excellent place to play archeologist or explorer for the day!

FLORENCE MARINA STATE PARK

Route 1, Box 36 (16 miles west of Lumpkin at the end of Ga 39C)

Omaha 31821

- Phone: (229) 838-6870, **Web: www.gastateparks.org**
- Hours: 7:00am-10:00pm
- Admission: FREE. Fee for camping and cottages.

This park offers the perfect setting for those who love water sports. It is adjacent to a natural deep-water marina with an accessible deep-water fishing pier, boat slips and boat ramp. The park's Kirbo Interpretive Center teaches visitors about Native Americans, local history and nature, and it displays artifacts from the prehistoric Paleo-Indian period through the early 20th century. The park also offers camping, cottages, a swimming pool and 3/4 mile nature trail.

BUTTS MILL FARM

2280 Butts Mill Road

Pine Mountain 31822

- Phone: (706) 663-7400, **Web: www.buttsmillfarm.com**
- Hours: Daily 10:00am-5:00pm.
- Admission: $9.95 adult, $7.95 child (3-12). Horseback riding $20.00 extra.

Visit this fully operational farm with miniature golf, train rides, bungee bull rides, pony rides, cow milking, Wild West Playground, petting farm, Wild Animal exhibits (cougar, camel, lion, tiger and bears), and a seasonal swimming hole with waterslide and swings. Plan to get your money's worth by staying a half-day or so. Rides and events occur on a daily schedule. Barn dances and concerts on occasional weekends.

CALLAWAY GARDENS

PO Box 2000 (either I-85 or I-185, exit east on Hwy. 18 to The Gardens at Callaway), **Pine Mountain** 31822

- Phone: (706) 663-5187 or (800) 225-5292
  Web: www.callawayonline.com
- Hours: Daily 9:00am-5:00pm. Extended summer hours. Beach open seasonally Memorial Day weekend through mid-August plus Labor Day weekend. Butterfly Center open mid-March through October only.
- Admission: $13.00 adult, $10.00 military, $6.50 child (6-12).
- Miscellaneous: They offer accommodations in the Inn and Cottages (start around $100 per night). Summer Family Adventure: stay overnight for several days and sign up for bike hikes (up to 10 miles long), storytelling, campfires, theme dinner, arts & crafts, Discovery programs, tours, circus performances, adventure challenge on the ropes course, aerobics, water skiing, Callaway Olympics, movies, bingo, and trail hikes (easy .5 to 1.2 mile trails).

There are so many activities offered that you never could do them all in one day. The Gardens offer a rock wall garden, sculpture garden, fern grotto, floral conservatory, Vegetable Garden, Pioneer life Log Cabin, hiking and biking trails, Robin Lake Beach (world's largest man-made, white sand beach), and Iceberg Island Floating Water Playground. Also within the property is: BIRDS OF PREY: The mighty birds of prey featured in these outdoor, free-flighted shows, demonstrate their strength, speed and natural instincts at a lakeside amphitheater that allows the creatures to swoop directly over spectators' heads. BUTTERFLY CENTER:

1,000 tropical butterflies, representing more than 50 different species, flutter freely through the air. North America's largest, glass-enclosed tropical conservatory. "On Wings of Wonder", plays continuously in the Center's orientation theater, explaining the life cycle of butterflies.

F. D. ROOSEVELT STATE PARK

2970 Georgia Highway 190 (I-185 near Callaway, west of Warm Springs on GA 190, or south of Rine Mountain off US 27)

Pine Mountain 31822

- Phone: (706) 663-4858 park or (877) 696-4613 stables
  Web: www.gastateparks.org
- Hours: Daily 7:00am-10:00pm.
- Admission: FREE

This park is deeply rooted in the historical era of four-time President Franklin D. Roosevelt. Seeking a place for treatment after he was stricken with polio in 1921, he traveled to the "curing" springs of the area and built a house. Several structures within the park, including the stone swimming pool, were built by the Civilian Conservation Corps during the Great Depression. Dowdell's Knob, Roosevelt's favorite picnic spot overlooking a magnificent view of the valley below is special. Hikers will enjoy the scenic trails (37 miles of) in the state's largest park. Camping, cottages, fishing, boating and horseback riding (stables, horse rentals, and 20 miles of trails) are here, too.

WILD ANIMAL SAFARI

1300 Oak Grove Road (I-185 North to Exit 42. Head east. Go approximately 6.7 miles), **Pine Mountain** 31822

- Phone: (706) 663-8744 or (800) 367-2751
  Web: www.animalsafari.com
- Hours: Daily 10:00am-5:30pm. Extended evening hours late spring thru summer. Closed Christmas day.

Wild Animal Safari *(cont.)*

- ❑ Admission: $11.95-$13.95 (age 3+). If you prefer to park your car but want to stay with your family, you may rent a park van for $10 for a 7 passenger mini van or $13.50 for a 15 passenger full size van in addition to regular ticket price.

See, feed and touch hundreds of exotic animals in this 500-acre park. Take a guided Zebra Bus or motor your own vehicle past giraffes or through the "Rhino Riviera". Upon entering the drive-through section, you immediately begin to see animals that come right to the vehicle and see others in the distance that give you the feeling of being on a safari in the Serengeti. After your tour of the Park, visit Old McDonald's Farm which is similar to a "zoo environment". The animals are penned and viewed from a walk through setting. The farm consists of the Monkey House, Alligator Pit, Petting Zoo, Tropical Bird section, Georgia Wildlife Museum and Baby Land USA.

ROCK RANCH

5020 Barnesville Hwy (I-75 south to exit 201. Take Hwy 36 west through town about 8 miles)

The Rock 30385

- ❑ Phone: (706) 647-6374, **Web: www.therockranch.com**
- ❑ Tours: $6.00 each for students and non-teaching adults. Teachers are FREE. All Field Trips are available Tuesdays thru Fridays 10:00am or 11:30am (Spring, Summer or Fall). Each tour includes a hayride of the ranch.
- ❑ Miscellaneous: Don't forget to wear your farm attire - wear old shoes, dress comfortably and for the weather. Bring a sack lunch to enjoy at the pavilion before returning home.

The Rock Ranch is a 750-acre working cattle farm, owned by S. Truett Cathy, founder of Chick-fil-A. They offer many seasonal events (see Seasonal & Special Events Chapter) and other "agritainment" or field trips. Some of the group tours available are: What's in a Farm? Learn about different animals in FarmLand...which of them have rectangular pupils, which ones can see in color? Let the goats entertain you on The Great Goat Walk. Pond Adventure! A pond is a really fun place to be in the spring. Learn about the delicate web of life and what we can do to preserve it, and the importance of conserving our wetlands. You'll dip your net into the water and examine dragonfly nymphs and other aquatic creatures under microscopes. Nature Hike - Observe animals and plants in their natural habitats. Watch the master builders and woodcutters at work, and search for the shy critters who like to hide! Pilgrim to Pioneer Days - Meet Pilgrims, dressed in period attire, and discover how they lived, and what they ate. Learn the relationship Native Americans had with these early settlers, and how those relationships shaped our country's early history. Students will meet and feed Farmland animals and learn how to care for them.

SPREWELL BLUFF STATE PARK

740 Sprewell Bluff Road (10 miles west of town. From GA 74 turn on Old Alabama Road and go south)

Thomaston 30286

- Phone: (706) 646-6026, **Web: www.gastateparks.org**
- Hours: Daily 7:00am- Sunset.
- Admission: FREE

Visitors can cool off in the gently flowing river, skip rocks across the water, picnic on the river's edge or toss horseshoes in a grassy field. A three-mile trail winds along a bank and up rocky bluffs, offering excellent views from high above the river. A boat ramp is available for canoeists, kayakers, rafters and fishermen. Canoes may be rented from several nearby outfitters, and camping is available 25 miles away at F. D. Roosevelt State Park in Pine Mountain.

LITTLE WHITE HOUSE HISTORIC SITE

401 Little White House Road (1/4 mile south of Warm Springs on GA 85 Alt - Hwy 27 Alt)

Warm Springs 31830

- Phone: (706) 655-5870, **Web: www.gastateparks.org**
- Hours: Daily 9:00am-4:45pm. Last full tour at 4:00pm.
- Admission: $4.00-$7.00

Franklin Delano Roosevelt first came to Warm Springs in 1924 hoping to find a cure for the infantile paralysis (polio) that had struck him in 1921. Swimming in the warm, buoyant spring waters brought him no miracle cure, but it did bring improvement. He built the Little White House in 1932 while governor of New York, prior to being inaugurated as president in 1933. During FDR's presidency and the Great Depression, he developed many New Deal Programs based upon his experiences in this small town. The newly updated facility has a number of Mr. Roosevelt's personal mementos. While posing for a portrait in April, 1945, FDR suffered a stroke and died a short while later. Today, the "Unfinished Portrait" is featured along with the President's 1938 Ford convertible with hand controls. Fireside Chats play over a 1930s radio and there is also a theatre. Visitors can tour FDR's home (looks like he just left it), the servants and guest quarters, and the nearby pools complex that first brought the future president to Warm Springs.

MUSEUM OF AVIATION/ GEORGIA AVIATION HALL OF FAME

GA Hwy 247 S and Russell Pkwy. (I-75 exit 146. Take US 247C to Robins Air Force Base)

Warner Robins 31099

- Phone: (478) 926-6870 or (888) 807-3359
  Web: www.museumofaviation.org
- Hours: Daily 9:00am-5:00pm except Thanksgiving Day,
- Christmas Day and New Year's Day.
- Admission: FREE
- Miscellaneous: Victory Café. Freedom Park playground and picnic pavilion area.

This huge, ever-updated museum includes historical displays of military aircraft and the aviation pioneers who "kept them flying" for freedom around the world. Different buildings or hangars house exhibits on artifacts, aircraft, missiles and engines. Many especially like the Vistascope Theater, "We the People" Theatre and the Presidential and combat helicopters or wartime planes. With names like "Blackbird" and "Dragon Lady", this place appeals to a sense of freedom and strength. Try to catch a presentation, demonstration (posted daily at the reception area) or "dress-up" flight area.

SUGGESTED LODGING AND DINING

COURTYARD BY MARRIOTT, **Macon** - 3990 Sheraton Drive (I-75 exit 169), 478-477-8899. Unwind and relax in one of the 108 spacious and comfortable guest rooms available at this hotel that features large sitting areas, spacious work desks, coffee makers, voice mail, and high speed Internet access in all of the rooms. Amenities on site include a restaurant, a lounge, a seasonal outdoor pool, an indoor whirlpool, an exercise room, guest laundry facilities, and meeting rooms. A breakfast buffet is served daily for around $8.00/$4.00. Just 2 exits north (I-75 exit 172) is Starcadia Entertainment Complex. **www.starcadia.net**. They have go-karts, mini-golf, bumper boats, batting cages, arcade, flying swings, junior go-karts, rock climbing, trampoline and even a couple of kiddie rides. Each activity averages around $5.00 per person (or 3 for $12.00).

NU-WAY WEINERS, MACON - 428 Cotton Avenue, downtown Macon, **www.nu-wayweiners.com** (478) 743-6593. Nu-Way has been serving up the best hot dogs in Macon for 87 years through three generations of the same family. Recently cited as being among the top 10 in the nation, these Central Georgia restaurants serve up secret-recipe chili sauce and homemade slaw. (10 other locations, include Zebulon Road at I-475; Northside Drive near I-75 and North Avenue at I-16). Hours: 6:00am-7:00pm. Breakfast, lunch and supper. Closed: Sunday. Price range: Under $5.00 for a complete lunch. A delectable selection of hot dog toppings, hamburgers, sandwiches and old fashioned chocolate malts can be enjoyed while sitting at a nostalgic stainless lunch counter or booth in the original downtown eatery or at one of ten other locations throughout Macon and Middle Georgia. Kids meals are served in "Dog Houses" and include a treat and toy. For about $1.39, you can order their signature red-colored hot dogs "all the way" - the best way is Nu-Way. Yum!

Chapter 3
North East Area - (NE)

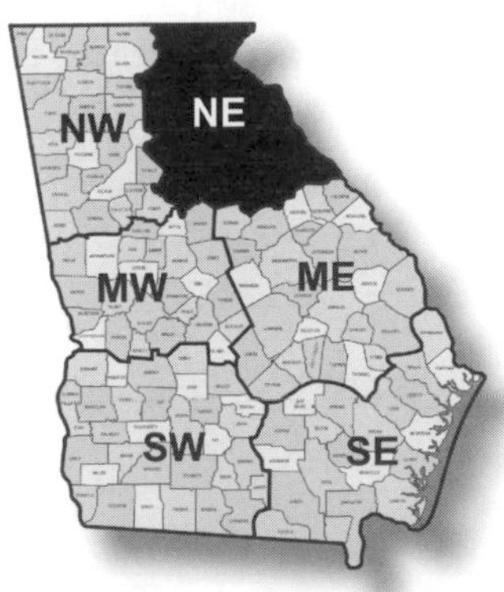

Our Favorites...

* Cabbage Patch Kids Babyland - Cleveland

* Gold Museum & Mines - Dahlonega

* Kangaroo Conservation Center - Dawsonville

* Lake Lanier Islands & Resort - Lake Lanier

* Northeast Georgia Waterfalls

There's Gold in the Hills!

UNIVERSITY OF GEORGIA

Four Towers Building, College Stadium Road

Athens 30602

- Phone: (706) 542-0842, **www.uga.edu/profile/visit.html**
- Hours: Visitors Center Info: Monday-Friday 8:00am-5:00pm, Saturday 9:00am-5:00pm, Sunday 1:00-5:00pm. Closed on UGA holidays.
- Admission: FREE
- Tours: Self-guided, or call for guided tours.

Some attactions include:

- BUTTS-MEHRE HERITAGE HALL & SPORTS MUSEUM - One Selig Circle, (706) 542-9036 or **www.georgiadogs.com**. Here, in the rotunda under the domed roof, are many exhibits and memorabilia tracing the long and proud heritage of all Georgia's athletic programs. In addition, recently upgraded touch-screen displays containing video highlights of Georgia's football history offer the chance to relive great Bulldog moments. (Call for hours)
- ITA COLLEGIATE TENNIS HALL OF FAME - UGA South Campus, (706) 542-8064 or **www.uga.edu/uga/bottom-va.html**. Famous inductees include Arthur Ashe, Jimmy Connors, and Stan Smith. (Monday-Friday 9:00am-Noon, 2:00-5:00pm)
- GEORGIA MUSEUM OF ART - 90 Carlton Street. (706) 542-4662 or **www.uga.edu/gamuseum**. Their permanent collection focuses on 19th-and early-20th century American paintings. Just My Imagination Workshops provide adults and their children a chance to create art together. The workshops are led by artists from Georgia and are free to participants. (Tuesday-Saturday 10:00am-5:00pm, Wednesday until 9:00pm, Sunday 1:00-5:00pm)

University of Georgia *(cont.)*

- STATE BOTANICAL GARDEN OF GEORGIA - 2450 South Milledge Avenue, (706) 542-1244 or **www.uga.edu/botgarden**. The three-story tropical conservatory dominates this 313-acre preserve. (Daily 8:00am to dusk)
- HORTICULTURE TRIAL GARDEN - 1111 Plant Science Building, Dept. of Horticulture, (706) 542-2471. Ornamental plants are performance-tested in seasonally rotating gardens. (Daily 8:00am-dusk)
- OCONEE FOREST PARK - UGA Recreational Sports Complex, College Station & E. Campus Roads, (706) 542-1571 or **www.forestry.uga.edu/warnell/ofp/**. Home to the Tree Trail, a network of trails with more than 100 native Georgia trees and shrubs identified by tags. The forest park also has lakeshore hiking, mountain bike trails, and a picnic area. (Daily 8:00am to dusk)

MEMORIAL PARK AND BEAR HOLLOW WILDLIFE TRAIL

293 Gran Ellen Drive (one street north of the East Campus Drive traffic light. Memorial Park is about two blocks down)

Athens 30606

- Phone: (706) 613-3580 or (706) 613-3616 zoo
  Web: www.athensclarkecounty.com/~bearhollow/
- Hours: Tuesday-Sunday 9:00am-5:00pm. Trails open until dark.
- Admission: FREE, donations accepted.
- Tours: Every Sunday they offer either guided feeding tours or a classroom project.

Wear your tennis shoes to experience 80 acres of rolling hills, a lake, walking trails, picnic spots, a playground area, and a small zoo. Resident animals include black bears, owls, otters, deer and bobcats. Keep your eyes and ears open and you may see the resident pair of red-shouldered hawks flying in the tree tops overhead.

SANDY CREEK NATURE CENTER AND ENSAT CENTER

205 Old Commerce Road (exit the 10 loop at 441 N)

Athens 30607

- Phone: (706) 613-3615,
  Web: www.sandycreeknaturecenter.com
- Hours: Tuesday-Saturday 8:30am-5:30pm.
- Admission: FREE

Explore over 225 acres of woodland, marshland, and fields that support a variety of wildlife along five miles of trails. Check out beavers at the clay pit pond. See ruins of a turn-of-the-century brick factory and an 1800's log house. Visit the Oconee River and Sandy Creek. Walk the Greenway or Cook's Trail. The ENSAT (Environment, Natural Science and Appropriate Technology) Center features live animal exhibits and wheelchair accessible trails. Meet a live sea turtle. Delve into an interactive wetlands exhibit complete with microscopes and a beaver lodge. View live venomous snakes from our region and other non-venomous species. Use the resource library to learn about natural science and ecology. Create nature crafts in the children's classroom or enjoy a story in the reading loft.

BRASSTOWN BALD

4811 Teague Road (tracing State Hwys 348, 180 and 17/75)

Blairsville 30512

- Phone: (706) 896-2556, **Web: www.fs.fed.us/conf**
- Hours: Daily (Memorial Day - October). Weekends only (March-May).
- Admission: $2.00 per car admission into Anna Ruby Falls parking lot.

Georgia's highest mountain, visitors can enjoy spectacular 360 degree views at an elevation point of 4,784 feet above sea level (Georgia's highest). To reach the bald's summit, families can either hike a half-mile trail or take a shuttle from the parking lot. A visitor's center is located at the top of the mountain along the 41.5 miles loop of the Russell-Brasstown Scenic Byway. On a clear day, you can see Atlanta. Seasonal activities include kite-making, wood-carving and mountain music festivals. It includes picnicking as well as an observation deck.

MISTY MOUNTAIN MODEL RAILROAD

4381 Misty Mountain Lane on Town Creek Road

Blairsville 30512

- Phone: (706) 745-9819
- Admission: $3.00 donation requested.
- Tours: One hour tour begins promptly at 2:00pm every Wednesday, Friday and Saturday (May-December).

America's largest o-gauge train display, the 3,400 square foot layout features 14 O-gauge Lionel trains traveling on a mile of track over 12 bridges and four trestles and through 15 tunnels. Many displays represent North Georgia and Atlanta.

TRACKROCK ARCHAEOLOGICAL AREA

(located on Trackrock Gap Road)

Blairsville 30512

- Phone: (706) 745-5493, **Web: www.fr.fed.us/conf**

This 52 acre area contains preserved petroglyphs of ancient Indian origin with carvings resembling animal and bird tracks, crosses, circles, and human footprints. Look for the historical marker. This park is open daily and is FREE.

VOGEL STATE PARK

7485 Vogel State Park Road (11 miles south of Blairsville via US 19-129), **Blairsville** 30512

- Phone: (706) 745-2628, **Web: www.gastateparks.org**
- Hours: Daily 7:00am-10:00pm.
- Admission: FREE. Fee for camping.

Vogel is located at the base of BLOOD MOUNTAIN in the Chattahoochee National Forest. Most popular in the fall, when the Blue Ridge Mountains transform into a rolling blanket of red, yellow and gold leaves. Cottages, campsites and primitive backpacking sites provide overnight accommodations. HELTON CREEK FALLS Trail (.3 mile in length) follows Helton Creek to two waterfalls. The trail accesses the lower falls at both the bottom and top of the falls and ends at the bottom of the upper falls. The total vertical drop is more than 100 feet. The rocks are deceptively slippery around these falls. Exercise caution! Go 2.2 miles to a small pullout parking area. Trailhead will be on the right. Outdoor activities include 17 miles of hiking to the falls (Appalachian Trail also nearby), fishing, swimming, pedal boat rental and miniature golf.

NORTHEAST GEORGIA WATERFALLS

Blairsville/Clarksville 30512

- **Web: www.visitnortheastgeorgia.com/waterfalls.htm**

Only a few waterfalls are visible from the road or parking lots. But most waterfalls can be easily reached, requiring varying lengths of walks or hikes.

DESOTO FALLS (Chestatee Ranger District) ~ There are five beautiful waterfalls located in the 650-acre recreation area. Three of these falls are maintained for the hiker's viewing convenience and are designated as the lower, middle, and upper DeSoto Falls. DeSoto Falls got its name from a legend that tells of a piece of armor found near the falls. It was decided that the armor belonged to Hernando DeSoto or one of his fellow explorers. Directions: From Cleveland, take U.S. 129 north 15 miles to DeSoto Falls Recreation Area.

PANTHER CREEK FALLS (Chattooga Ranger District) ~ Panther Creek Falls Trail (5.5 miles in length) follows Panther Creek through stands of hemlock and white pine along steep, rocky bluffs of the creek. The trail passes a series of cascades, as well as, the falls. Directions: From Clarkesville, take U.S. 23/441 north for 10 miles to the Panther Creek Recreation Area. (706) 754-6221. Admission: $2.00 per vehicle.

BLUE RIDGE SCENIC RAILWAY

241 Depot Street (I-575 north to town. Turn right at second light. Follow signs to railroad tracks)

Blue Ridge 30513

- Phone: (706) 632-9833 or (800) 934-1898
  Web: www.brscenic.com

- Admission: $22.00-$26.00 adult, $18.00-$22.00 senior (65+), $11.00-$13.00 child (2-12). Advanced reservations recommended. Payment is required at time of booking. 48 hours notice required to cancel.
- Tours: Seasonal schedule with departures at 10:00am, 11:00am, 1:00pm or 2:30pm. Daily summers, mostly weekends spring and fall. (March through mid-November)
- Miscellaneous: Commissary car with snacks and souvenirs. Restrooms on board.

Rent a cabin, climb a mountain, hike a trail and ride the Blue Ridge Scenic Railway. The train route consists of a 26-mile round trip through historic Murphy Junction along the beautiful Toccoa River. This railroad was built over 100 years ago. Choose from vintage, climate controlled coaches or open air rail cars. Each trip includes a stop in McCaysville which permits passengers to stretch their legs while exploring the downtown shops of McCaysville, Georgia and Copperhill, Tennessee. The sister towns divided by the TN-GA state line have fresh mountain air and little eateries or ice cream shops for a treat or light lunch or snack. Each round trip takes approximately 3 1/2 hours.

MAYFIELD DAIRY FARMS

1160 Broadway Avenue (I-285 East to I-85 North. Turn right at Exit 126), **Braselton** 30517

- Phone: (706) 654-9180 or (888) 298-0396
  Web: www.mayfielddairy.com
- Hours: Monday-Friday 9:00am-5:00pm, Saturday 9:00am-2:00pm.
- Admission: FREE
- Tours: No tours on Wednesday. Weekday tours begin every 30 minutes. Saturday tours begin every hour. Last tour begins 1 hour before closing. No milk production on Wednesday or Saturday.

Mayfield Dairy Farms (cont.)

Get the "scoop" on the history of this dairy through a film presentation followed by a plant tour that includes how milk is bottled. Begin by watching all the swirling and twirling and spinning and turning and churning of jugs. The fun tour includes a great look at how they make plastic milk jugs from a handful of tiny pellets…melted and molded. See the Aro-Vac that removes unwanted flavors from milk or how they homogenize, pasteurize, and add vitamins to milk. After the guided visual tour - taste some of their ice cream creations for sale (cheap!). Try Snow Cream.

LANIER MUSEUM OF NATURAL HISTORY

2601 Buford Dam Road (located in the Department of Public Utilities Water Treatment Facility)

Buford 30518

- Phone: (770) 932-4460
- Hours: Tuesday-Saturday Noon-5:00pm.
- Admission: $1.00 per person (age 4+).

The Lanier Museum presents an overview of the natural world found in Gwinnett County and surrounding areas. Located south of Lake Lanier's Buford Dam, the museum houses a collection of live animals, replicated habitat exhibits, rocks and fossils, and more. We offer a wide variety of programs including environmental excursions, gardening, animals, fossils, and other environmental topics. Best to attend classes (extra fee) catering to your interests.

MOCCASIN CREEK STATE PARK

3655 Georgia Highway 197 (20 miles north of town on GA 197 or 15 miles west of Clayton via GA 76 and GA 197)

Clarkesville 30523

- Phone: (706) 947-3194, **Web: www.gastateparks.org**
- Hours: Daily 7:00am-10:00pm.
- Admission: FREE. Fee for camping.

Moccasin Creek is nestled in the Blue Ridge Mountains on the shores of Lake Burton. Despite its mountain location, the park is relatively flat, offering easy navigation for biking. A fully accessible fishing pier sits above a trout-filled creek open only to physically challenged visitors, senior citizens and children. Tour the adjacent trout rearing station or hike on several nearby mountain trails (2 mile Hemlock Falls Hiking Trail). The park also offers seasonal canoe and jon boat rentals.

TALLULAH GORGE STATE PARK

P O Box 248 (US 441)

Clayton (Tallulah Falls) 30525

- Phone: (706) 754-7970, **Web: www.gastateparks.org**
- Hours: Daily 8:00am-dark (park). Center hours 8:00am-5:00pm (plus $4.00 parking).
- Admission: FREE. Camping fees.
- Miscellaneous: Nantahala Outdoor Center (Chattooga Ridge Road, 864-638-5980 or 800-232-7238 or **www.noc.com**) offers white-water rafting and kayaking trips from Clayton.

Tallulah Gorge is two miles long and nearly 1,000 feet deep. Visitors can hike rim trails to several overlooks. Exhibits in the Interpretive Center highlight the history of the old Victorian resort town, as well as the geography and fragile ecosystem of the area. Additionally, the park has produced a film that takes viewers on the dramatic journey through the gorge. Some like to whitewater paddle (first two April weekends and first three November weekends). There are more than 20 miles of hiking and mountain biking trails and a separate 1.7 mile paved "Rails to Trails" path. Swimming and camping are available, too.

NORTHEAST GEORGIA WATERFALLS

Clayton/Helen 30525

- Phone: (706) 782-3320 (Clayton) or (706) 754-6221 (Helen)
  Web: www.visitnortheastgeorgia.com/waterfalls.htm

Start close to downtown Clayton at Becky Branch Falls (Warwoman Road), a 20-foot cascade easily accessible with a walk up a trail to a bridge at the base of the falls. Dick's Creek Falls (off Sandy ford Road) is 60 feet high and makes a sheer drop over a granite mound into the Chattooga River. At the top, there's a viewing area. Finally, the Holcomb Creek Trail passes Holcomb Creek Falls (Hale Ridge Road), which drops and flows over the shoals for approximately 150 feet, and Ammons Creek Falls, where there is an observation deck. In Helen, there's Horse Trough Falls (GA 75 & Forest Service Rd 44) - follow the Falls Trail (.04 mile in length) leading to the beautiful falls. Also, the Raven Cliff Falls (off Russell-Brasstown Scenic Byway) - perhaps one of the most unusual in the area because the water flows through a split in the face of a solid rock outcropping and plummets to the ground 100 feet below.

CABBAGE PATCH KIDS BABYLAND

73 W. Underwood Street) (GA 129, downtown - look for the signs)

Cleveland 30528

- Phone: (706) 865-2171, **Web: www.cabbagepatchkids.com**
- Hours: Monday-Saturday 9:00am-5:00pm, Sunday 10:00am-5:00pm.
- Admission: FREE

Enter the Babyland General Hospital, birthplace of the Cabbage Patch Kids and home to original artist Xavier Roberts' creations from the early 80s to now. Walk into the magical Cabbage Patch town starting in the nursery, then to the school house and playgrounds. Don't you just love their adorable hair? Licensed Patch Nurses and Doctors are on call to assist Mother Cabbages in labor and provide advice for on-site adoptive parents. When you hear a nurse call "Delivery Room STAT!" you need to hurry to the Patch. Here, you'll witness the birth of a one-of-a-kind, soft Cabbage Patch Kid. Wander through the rest of the "Hospital" gift shop and maybe fall in love with a baby and adopt it to take home. Fun is born here!

WATSON MILL BRIDGE STATE PARK

650 Watson Mill Road (3 miles south of Comer off GA 22)

Comer 30629

- Phone: (706) 783-5349, **Web: www.gastateparks.org**
- Hours: Daily 7:00am-10:00pm.
- Admission: FREE. Fee for camping.

Watson Mill Bridge contains the longest original-site covered bridge in the state, spanning 229 feet across the South Fork River. Built in 1885, the bridge is supported by a town lattice truss system held firmly together with wooden pins. Hiking (7 miles), biking (5 miles) and horseback riding (12 miles) trails allow visitors to enjoy the thick forest along the river or travel into the park's backcountry. During summer, kids often play in the cool river shoals just below the bridge.

CHARLIE ELLIOTT WILDLIFE CENTER

543 Elliott Trail (I-20 east to Exit 98, south on Georgia Highway 11, Monroe-Monticello)

Covington (Mansfield) 31064

- Phone: (770) 784-3059, **Web: www.monticelloga.org**
- Hours: Tuesday-Saturday 9:00am-4:30pm. Sunday 1:00-4:30pm (April-October only)
- Admission: FREE

The property has dozens of ponds with a large rock outcropping. Activities include hiking, fishing, birdwatching, archery, and primitive camping. Visitors Center and Museum.

A. H. STEPHENS STATE HISTORIC PARK

P O Box 310 (north of I-20 exit 148 and go north on GA 22 for 2 miles. Then, go east on US 278)

Crawfordville 30631

- Phone: (706) 456-2602, **Web: www.gastateparks.org**
- Hours: Park: 7:00am-10:00pm. Historic Site: Tuesday-Saturday 9:00am-5:00pm, Sunday 2:00-5:00pm. Closed Monday except holidays.
- Admission: $1.50-$3.00 Historic site

This site combines recreation with education. Named after the vice president of the Confederacy and governor of Georgia. The park features a Confederate museum with one of the finest collections of Civil War artifacts in the state, including uniforms and documents. Stephen's home, Liberty Hall, is renovated to its 1875 style, fully furnished and open for tours. There are cottages, campgrounds and large overnight group camps.

CONSOLIDATED GOLD MINE

185 Consolidated Gold Mine Road (main crossroad of town where US 19, GA 60, GA 9 & GA 52 run together - the mine is under the Walmart)

Dahlonega 30533

- Phone: (706) 864-8473,
  Web: www.consolidatedgoldmine.com
- Hours: Daily 10:00am-4:00pm (winter) or 5:00pm (summer).
- Admission: $11.00 adult, $7.00 child (4-14). Includes gold panning.
- Tours: Tours are guided and run daily year-round. Your tour guides are open to questions and welcome interaction during the 40-45 minute tour. The mines remain at a comfortable 60 degrees year round.

Thar's gold in them *thar* hills! This authentic mine site offers underground tours of a hard rock gold mine and gold panning. Once in the massive underground network of tunnels (complete with the original track system), you'll learn about techniques used by early miners. Hear a loud air hammer drill bit demonstrated! The tour introduces guests to the geology of the gold belt including the quartz and pyrite formation which early miners were working at the turn of the century. Amazingly, you can still find gold in these hills! Look for it underground. Once you're done with the geology tour, try your hand at gold panning using techniques you just learned about.

CRISSON GOLD MINE

2736 Morrison Moore Parkway East (2 1/2 miles north of town on US 19 Connector)

Dahlonega 30533

- Phone: (706) 864-6363
- Hours: Daily (except Christmas) 10:00am-6:00pm.
- Admission: Yes, call for latest prices.

Gold was first discovered in the Dahlonega area in 1828, twenty years before the Gold Rush to California. When it was discovered it was completely by accident – when a deer hunter, Benjamin Parks, tripped over a rock 2½ miles south of what is now Dahlonega. Upon inspecting the rock, he discovered that it was full of gold! Within one year's time, some 15,000 miners heard about that and rushed to find some gold for themselves. At that time there was so much gold in and around Dahlonega that it laid on top of the ground, washing off the mountainsides for centuries. The Crisson Gold Mine, dating back to 1847, is open for tours and gold panning. The operating 10-stamp mill is demonstrated as part of the Crisson Gold Mine Tour. Pan for gold or try you luck at gem grubbin', where you can find rubies, emeralds, garnets, and more.

DAHLONEGA GOLD MUSEUM HISTORIC SITE

#1 Public Square (Public Square in town, 5 miles west of GA 400)

Dahlonega 30533

- Phone: (706) 864-2257, **Web: www.gastateparks.org**
- Hours: Monday-Saturday 9:00am-5:00pm, Sunday 10:00am-5:00pm. Closed major winter holidays.
- Admission: $1.50-$3.00 per person.

- Miscellaneous: Gold Rush packages include discounted tickets and a gold panning dish. The friendly Welcome Center offers directions and tickets (located in the town square).

Many years before the Gold Rush out west, thousands of gold seekers flocked into the Cherokee Nation in North Georgia. In the mid-1800s, more than $6 million in gold was coined by the US Mint. Located in the old county courthouse, this museum tells the story of the mining history of Georgia and displays many large gold nuggets and coins. A 23-minute film describes the mining techniques and lifestyles of the prospectors through interviews with mining families. Look at and discover what a stamp machine is. Or, what is a water cannon and why was it so hclpful to miners? Gold now can be processed so thin, it looks like paper. Very interesting and educational.

AMICALOLA FALLS STATE PARK AND LODGE

240 Amicalola Falls State Park Road (Hwy 53 west to Hwy 183 north to Hwy 52 east. 15 miles NW of town)

Dawsonville 30534

- Phone: (706) 265-4703 or 265-8888 (lodge)
  Web: www.gastateparks.org
- Hours: Daily 7:00am-10:00pm.

Amicalola is a Cherokee Indian word meaning "tumbling waters" - an appropriate name for the 729-foot falls - the tallest east of the Mississippi River. Numerous trails are available for short journeys. The lodge is popular with guests who prefer hotel-like comforts (private porches with breathtaking glass-walled views) but they also offer cottages and camping. A 5-mile hike leads to more remote accommodations at the Len Foote Hike Inn. Accommodations run $60.00-$160.00 per night and the lodge has a restaurant. The park office has nature displays, live creature exhibits and a gift shop.

KANGAROO CONSERVATION CENTER

222 Bailey-Waters Road (GA 400 north to GA 136 west 12 miles, turn right on Bailey-Waters. Or, I-75 to US76 east to GA 52 east)

Dawsonville 30534

- Phone: (706) 265-6100, **Web: www.kangaroocenter.com**
- Admission: $27.50 adult, $22.50 child (8-18).
- Tours: Guided 2 hour tours in a 10-wheel drive truck available Tuesday, Thursday and Saturday, by reservation only. Must be age 8+. Spring through Fall.
- Miscellaneous: Some optional parts of your tour require walking on nature trails with some steep slopes. Please wear appropriate footwear. Since much of the tour is outside, bring a hat and/or raincoat as needed. Smoking is not permitted on the grounds.

Ride through the "Outback" and view the largest collection of kangaroos outside Australia. This large zoological park is located in the mountains and the behind-the-scenes tour teaches about animal care while the kids meet wildlife face to face. This is not a petting zoo, but a working animal farm providing zoological animals worldwide. Begin your tour out in the field learning to toss a boomerang - yes, everyone gets to try. Next, your guides will explain many aspects of kangaroo behavior. In the arena, various animals will take turns visiting (actually, running around) with you in the arena as they "check you out". What do you notice? See their strong tails? Want to pet one? You can! Just like us, they don't prefer to be petted on their face - but instead they like backrubs. Now, get on the open-air truck for a ride through the Outback. You might observe Moms teaching their young to play and "box". It's neat, as you gaze at them, they are curiously looking back at you, too. Types of animals you'll see are: Red Kangaroos, Grey Roos, Burros, Kookaburras, Wallabees, Cranes and Ducks. Lots of educational tidbits are wonderfully mixed into this amusing and interesting tour! Something we recommend "hopping" over to...

THUNDER ROAD USA - GEORGIA RACING HALL OF FAME

415 Hwy 53 east (GA 400 exit Hwy 53 west)

Dawsonville 30534

- Phone: (706) 216-RACE, **Web: www.thunderroadusa.com**
- Hours: Weekends 10:00am-5:00pm. Closed Christmas only.
- Admission: $6.50-$8.50 (age 6+). May be temporarily closed. Call or check website for latest details.

This museum's theme is realistic old streets, garages and race cars. Sit in old cars and on tailgates to view custom films on racing at the "Drive-in". Follow family and famous racing legends in the Hall of Fame. Race head-to-head on the largest indoor RC track in the USA with total car control - no slots. Ride Simulators beyond 200 mph and then cool down at the retro-racing diner treats to eat.

BOBBY BROWN STATE PARK

2509 Bobby Brown State Park (21 miles SE of Elberton off GA 72)

Elberton 30635

- Phone: (706) 213-2046, **Web: www.gastateparks.org**
- Hours: Daily 7:00am-10:00pm
- Admission: FREE
- Miscellaneous: Coming on GA 72 east from town, look for signs leading to Old Dan Tucker's Gravesite. Mr. Tucker is best known as the minister whose empathy for slaves inspired the American folk song by his name.

Bobby Brown State Park *(cont.)*

The park is named in memory of Lt. Robert T. Brown, U S Navy, who gave his life in World War II. When water levels are low, visitors can see some foundations of the old town that was once there and imagine large plantations flourishing. The park's strategic location on the largest man-made lake east of the Mississippi River provides excellent boating, skiing and fishing. New yurts (like tents but make of canvas and wood) offer a new way to camp. The park offers almost 2 miles of hiking trails, a seasonal swimming pool, and canoe, pedal or fishing boat rentals.

NANCY HART CABIN

River Road (off Highway 17, south of Elberton)

Elberton 30635

- Phone: (706) 283-5651
- Hours: Monday-Saturday 9:00am-5:00pm.
- Admission: FREE

During the American Revolution a party of British Tories came to Mrs. Hart's home. Single-handedly she killed one and wounded another. The remainder of the party surrendered and were later hanged by her and a few of her neighbors. A replica of her cabin, complete with gun holes is open to visitors. Call ahead and arrange a tour so you can hear the fabulous stories of how her size and character gained her notoriety as a colonial spy during the American Revolution.

RICHARD B. RUSSELL STATE PARK

2650 Russell State Park Road (8 miles northeast of town off GA 77 on Ruckersville Road),

Elberton 30635

- Phone: (706) 213-2045, **Web: www.gastateparks.org**
- Hours: Daily 7:00am-10:00pm.
- Admission: FREE. Camping and cottage fees.

This state park offers some of the state's finest fishing and boating. A nature trail follows the shoreline to one of the oldest steel pin bridges in the area, loops through the adjoining woods and returns to the beach. The park's campground and fully equipped cottages are located on or near the water's edge for relaxation. There are canoe and pedal boat rental and six miles of hiking and biking trails. Several Indian sites were excavated near the park in 1980 before the lake was filled, indicating that Paleo-Indians lived in the area more than 10,000 years ago. All Park facilities are designed for wheelchair accessibility, including the swimming beach.

ATLANTA FALCONS HEADQUARTERS AND TRAINING FACILITY

4400 Falcon Parkway (I-985 northeast)

Flowery Branch 30542

- Phone: (888) 965-3115
  Web: www.atlantafalcons.com/community/007/638/

Fans can watch most practices during Falcons Training Camp, which is held at the team's headquarters in Flowery Branch. In addition, the team usually has Rookie Mini Camp during the week following the NFL Draft. Each year at training camp (July and August) the team's practices are open and free to the public. Occasionally after practice, some fans will receive autographs from the players as they exit the field.

NORTHEAST GEORGIA HISTORY CENTER

322 Academy Street (Brenau University), **Gainesville** 30501

- Phone: (770) 536-0889, **Web: www.negahistorycenter.org**
- Hours: Tuesday-Friday 10:00am-4:00pm or by appointment.
- Admission: A small fee donation is charged.

This regional history museum includes a replica country store, artifacts from the 1996 Olympics, a "whirlwind" diorama of items that might have been tossed around in the 1936 Gainesville tornado, and a doctor's office from the 1940s. Another exhibit space highlights the drawings by Ed Dodd, creator of the Mark Trail comic strip.

ELACHEE NATURE SCIENCE CENTER

2125 Elachee Drive (I-985 exit 16 onto Mundy Mill Road, SR53. Follow signs to Elachee and SR 13 to Chicopee Woods area)

Gainesville 30504

- Phone: (770) 535-1976, **Web: www.elachee.org**
- Hours: Trails open 8:00am-dusk. Nature Center open daily (except Sunday) 10:00am-5:00pm.
- Admission: Trails are FREE. Center charges $2.00-$3.00 per person (age 2+).

Elachee's sprawling campus consists of a woodland refuge and an interactive museum that will excite and educate visitors of all ages. Visit animal exhibits and feel free to visit their "touch tables" to examine a selection of unique nature objects. Surrounding the Center is the 1,400 acre Chicopee Woods Nature Preserve laced with over 12 miles of nature trails. Their "Budding Naturalists" program introduces nature to 3, 4 and 5 year olds and also increases parents' comfort level and knowledge in the out-of-doors. Songs, creative movement, crafts, storytelling, mini-hikes, visits with live animals, and learning about different nature topics each day are all part of the fun and adventure.

HART STATE PARK

330 Hart State Park Road (drive north of town on US 29, turn left on Ridge Road and proceed 2 miles to the park)

Hartwell 30643

- Phone: (706) 376-8756, **Web: www.gastateparks.org**
- Hours: Daily 7:00am-10:00pm.
- Admission: FREE. Fee for camping and cottages.

The park's boat ramps and docks offer easy access to all water sports. Swimming, boating, water skiing and fishing at Lake Hartwell are the prime reasons folks visit this park. A swimming beach and picnic tables along with cottages and most campsites are located on the scenic lake shore. There are canoe, jon boat and pontoon boat rentals and a short hiking and biking trail.

ALPINE AMUSEMENT PARK

419 Edelweiss Strasse

Helen 30545

- Phone: (706) 878-2306
- Hours: Daily 1:00-11:00pm (summers). Weekends only (March-May & September-November).
- Admission: Depends on rides.

They boast Go-Carts and the largest bumper boat pool in Georgia. Combine this with old-time, nostalgic rides like the tilt-a-whirl, an Eli #5 ferris wheel, the roll-a-plane and an 18-hole miniature golf course. There are 5 kiddie rides including gas powered carts and a rare pre-World War II miniature train. The park also has batting cages, an arcade, remote controlled boats, and the Water Wars water balloon game.

ALPINE ANTIQUE AUTO AND BUGGY MUSEUM

115 Escowee Drive (one block from SR 75, left onto Hamby Street, cross bridge and take first right)

Helen 30545

- Phone: (706) 878-0072, **Web: www.alpinemuseum.com**
- Hours: Daily 10:00am-6:00pm.
- Admission: $5.00

Antique cars from the early 1900's through the late 1970's - Many from the collection of Jessie James. Look for Muscle Cars, Street Rods, over 100 Horse Drawn Buggies, a US Army Civil War Ambulance, a late 1800s Mail Wagon and Water Wagon. They even have more modern cars from country stars like Minnie Pearl or Little Jimmy Dickens.

BLACK FOREST BEAR PARK AND REPTILE EXHIBIT

8160 South Main Street, **Helen** 30545

- Phone: (706) 878-7043
- Hours: Monday-Friday 10:00am-7:00pm, Saturday 10:00am-8:00pm, Sunday 11:00am-6:00pm.
- Admission: $4.00 per person.

This park educates people about many different species of bears commonly found in the state of Georgia. Some of the species you will observe are the American Black Bear, Grizzly Bear, Himalayan Bear, Syrian Brown Bear, and others. At each exhibit, there is a map showing where they live and some detailed information about each species. Not only do you get to see these animals up close, but you get to feed them as well. The reptile exhibit has numerous types of large snakes for observation including all the poisonous snakes found in this country. The owners of the park have over 10 years of experience in breeding and keeping animals alive. Many of these bears would be destroyed because of no more use in circuses or they are troubled bears, such as raiding campgrounds.

CHARLEMAGNE'S KINGDOM

8808 North Main Street

Helen 30545

- Phone: (706) 878-2200,
  Web: www.georgiamoderailroad.com
- Hours: Daily 10:00am-6:00pm.
- Admission: $2.50-$5.00 per person.

Charlemagne's Kingdom is an Alpine Model railroad layout, in HO scale miniature. All of the buildings are replicas of buildings existing in Germany, over five thousand hand painted figures, 400' of railroad track, computerized trains, and hot air balloons, three ring circus, mountains 22' tall, and much more. While you are here, watch the Glockenspiel dancer in the Gingerbread House (dances occur at Noon, 3:00pm & 6:00pm).

HORNE'S BUGGY RIDES

165 Dandy Lane (corner of River and Main Street in downtown)

Helen 30545

- Phone: (706) 878-3658
  Web: www.helenga.org/hornesbuggyrides
- Admission: $5.00 adult, $3.00 child.

Buggy rides through the streets of Helen, an old Bavarian town. Pictures with the horse, King George and his canine companion, Cap'n Jim are welcome.

REMEMBER WHEN THEATRE

115 Escowee Drive (one block from SR 75, near Main Street)

Helen 30545

- Phone: (706) 878-SHOW
  Web: www.rememberwhentheatre.com
- Hours: Shows start at 8:00pm. Doors open at 7:00pm. Concessions at 6:30pm.
- Admission: $16.00 adult, $8.00 child (under 12).

Mark Pitt currently performs every Saturday night at The Remember When Theatre in Helen, which was specifically built in 2001 for Mark's "Tribute to Elvis" show. "Elvis" is known to spoil the kids by throwing out teddy bears and the moms by giving scarves to all the ladies. Mark Pitt, an exciting Entertainer, captivates the heart and soul of Elvis Presley on stage. He brings back wonderful memories of America's most loved and missed entertainer.

SMITHGALL WOODS - DUKES CREEK CONSERVATION AREA

61 Tsalaki Trail (on GA 75A, 3 miles west of town, just south of GA 348), **Helen** 30545

- Phone: (706) 878-3087, **Web: www.gastateparks.org**
- Hours: Daily 7:00am-6:00pm.
- Admission: FREE. Fee for camping and cottages.

A premier trout stream, Dukes Creek runs through the mountain property and is a favorite for catch-and-release fishing. Four miles of trails and 18 miles of roads allow hikers and bicyclists to explore the woods, wildlife and streams. Van tours are offered daily at 12:30pm. The Lodge at Smithgall Woods is an elegant mountain retreat perfect for getaways. Five cottages provide 14 bedrooms with private baths (rates include accommodations, meals and activities). Reservations are required for trout fishing.

UNICOI STATE PARK AND LODGE

P O Box 849 (2 miles northeast of Helen via GA 356)

Helen 30545

- Phone: (706) 878-2201 (lodge) or (706) 878-0983 (programs) **Web: www.gastateparks.org**
- Hours: Daily 7:00am-10:00pm.

Guests will find a variety of activities including swimming, fishing hiking, biking, wildlife viewing or relaxing in the Lodge's retreat-like atmosphere or in one of the numerous cottages or campsites. Outdoor enthusiasts will enjoy hiking and biking on scenic mountain trails, especially those leading to Helen and ANNA RUBY FALLS. Named by landowner John Nichols for his last living family member, daughter Anna Ruby, the falls form a twin cascade into Smith Creek. The visitor center has a viewing deck where visitors can feed the trout. The Lodge provides a restaurant and the marina docks have canoe and pedal boat rentals.

CRYSTAL RIVER RANCH LLAMA TREKS

7316 US Hwy 76E

Hiawassee 30546

- Phone: (706) 896-5005, **Web: www.crystalriver-ranch.com**
- Tours: Treks depart from the ranch at 10:00am and usually last from 3 to 4 hours. Day Hike including lunch is $45.00 per person (24 hour advanced reservations).

Guided Day Hikes in the beautiful North Georgia mountains without carrying all of the necessities. Llamas will be your trail companions while you enjoy the scenery, exercise, and fresh mountain air. This leisurely, 2.5 mile trek in the Chattahoochee National Forest goes through tall timber, clear mountain streams, and wildlife clearings. Along the way, they provide a hearty lunch on the trail. Something of a reward in the middle of the adventure.

HIGH SHOALS FALLS & SCENIC AREA

Forest Service Road (off GA 75 north to Indian Grave Gap Road, Service Road 283),

Hiawassee 30546

- Phone: (706) 745-6928, **Web: www.fs.fed.us/conf**
- Admission: FREE

Follow the creek hiking path to the viewing platform at two waterfalls. Open daily, be sure of weather conditions for hiking and driving to the trailheads. In winter with snow, often four-wheel drive vehicles are required.

CRAWFORD W. LONG MUSEUM

28 College Street (off US 129, in the heart of downtown)

Jefferson 30549

- Phone: (706) 367-5307, **Web: www.crawfordlong.org**
- Hours: Tuesday-Saturday 10:00am-4:00pm.
- Admission: Admission is FREE; donations are appreciated.

This is the site of the first painless surgery. Dr. Crawford W. Long was the physician who, on March 30, 1842, first used ether for surgical anesthesia. While yet a young doctor, he observed the frolicking actions of youth around him using ether to kill the pain of their recreation. Soon after, a patient requested he remove a cyst from the neck. Using ether, the operation was successful and the patient felt no pain. Personal artifacts of Dr. Long, as well as early anesthesia equipment are displayed in the Medical Museum. The antebellum Pendergrass Store Building houses a recreated 1840s doctor's office and apothecary shop. Exhibits on making medicine focus on the obstacles the early country doctor was forced to overcome. The building also includes a replica of a 19th century General Store and serves as the performance area for Museum programs such as storytelling, live music, craft and historical demonstrations. Take a stroll outside in the Knot Garden to learn the culinary and medicinal uses of the herbs and plants growing there.

LAKE LANIER ISLANDS

7000 Holiday Road (I-085 north, exit 8, then GA 347 west OR GA 400 north exit 14. Then, left on GA 20 for 10 miles, left on Peachtree and left again on Friendship Road)

Lake Lanier Islands 30518

- Phone: (770) 932-7200 or (800) 840-5253
  Web: www.lakelanierislands.com
- Hours: Waterpark: Daily 10:00am-6:00pm (late May thru August). Weekends only in September.
- Admission: Waterpark: $27.00 general, $17.00 senior and child (under 42" tall).

The Islands Resort is a year-round vacation spot located on the pristine southernmost shore of Lake Lanier. Accommodations include deluxe waterfront lake house rentals, hotel and a lakeside campground. A beach and water park, golf course, heated swimming pool, and boat rentals are available. WATER PARK - incredible FunDunker, with more than 100 ways to get wet! Hang Ten on the Surf Wave®; ride Wild Waves, Georgia's largest wave pool; and real thrill seekers go to extremes on the Intimidator, the Twister, SplashDown, and Triple Threat. Plus, the little ones will love Kiddie Lagoon and Wiggle Waves. Looking for a little R&R? Troubles melt away on their mile-long, sandy white beach. (Must be more than 42" tall to ride most slides. Must be 48" tall to ride the Surf Wave and FunDunker drop). Boating - from houseboats to pleasure cruising, they have gorgeous, large boats to rent on this beautiful lake. See separate listing for Lake Lanier Lakehouse Lodging at the end of this chapter.

TUGALOO STATE PARK

1763 Tugaloo State Park Road (I-85 exit 173 north on GA 17, follow park signs)

Lavonia 30533

- Phone: (706) 356-4352, **Web: www.gastateparks.org**
- Hours: Daily 7:00am-10:00pm.
- Admission: FREE. Fee for camping and cottages.

The name "Tugaloo" comes from an Indian name for the river which once flowed freely prior to the construction of Hartwell Dam. Tugaloo's cottages and camping offer spectacular views of Lake Hartwell. Some cottages even have private boat docks for overnight guests. Ten campers can choose modern or primitive campsites. Fishing is excellent and during the summer, the lake is a popular destination for swimming, water skiing, sailing and boating. Both the Crow Tree and Muscadine nature trails wind through oak, walnut, mulberry and cherry trees.

ELIJAH CLARK STATE PARK

2959 McCormick Highway (7 miles northeast of Lincolnton on US 378), **Lincolnton** 30817

- Phone: (706) 359-3458, **Web: www.gastateparks.org**
- Hours: Daily 7:00am-10:00pm.
- Admission: FREE

This park is named for a frontiersman and state war hero who led pioneers during the Revolutionary War. A renovated and furnished log cabin museum displays furniture, utensils and tools and is open for weekend only tours (April-November). Look for the graves of Clark and his wife, Hannah. The park is located on a large lake - cottages are located on the lake's edge, and the spacious campground is nestled into the forest. The park also offers hiking trails (3.75 miles), swimming, shuffleboard, and miniature golf.

BLACK ROCK MOUNTAIN STATE PARK

P O Drawer A (3 miles north of Clayton off US 441, follow signs)

Mountain City 30562

- Phone: (706) 746-2141, **Web: www.gastateparks.org**
- Hours: Daily 7:00am-10:00pm.
- Admission: FREE

Named for its sheer cliffs of dark-colored biotitic gneiss, this park encompasses some of the most outstanding country in Georgia's Blue Ridge Mountains. At an altitude of 3,640 feet, Black Rock Mountain is the highest state park in Georgia. Numerous scenic overlooks provide spectacular 80-mile vistas of the Southern Appalachians. Several hiking trails (10 miles worth) lead past wildflowers, streams, small waterfalls and full forests. There are also camping and cottage facilities plus the summit visitor center.

FOXFIRE MUSEUM

2839 US Hwy 441S (near US 441 & US 76 intersection, far northeast corner of GA)

Mountain City 30562

- Phone: (706) 746-5828, **Web: www.foxfire.org**
- Hours: Monday-Friday 8:30am-4:30pm. Closed holidays.
- Admission: $5.00 general (age 11+).
- Miscellaneous: The Museum also includes a scenic nature trail and cabins that are available for vacation rentals. A gift shop filled with folk art, handcrafted items, and books, including The Foxfire Book series, is located in the Gate House, the first log cabin you'll see on Foxfire Lane.

The Foxfire Museum focuses on Appalachian life and is rooted in the work that hundreds of regional high school students, in The Foxfire Magazine classes, have put into documenting their local history. Visitors see a glimpse of what life was like for the mountaineers who settled this area over 150 years ago as they tour over 20 historic log cabins. Buildings include a chapel, blacksmith shop, mule barn, wagon shed, single-room home, gristmill, and smokehouse. Included on the property is a wagon used in the Trail of Tears - the forced Cherokee migration from these mountains to Oklahoma. Many of the cabins contain artifacts and crafts of early Appalachian life, including toys, wagons, cabin-building tools, blacksmithing instruments, woodworking tools, handmade items, household items, logging tools, shoemaking equipment, animal trapping and hunting equipment, and farm and agricultural equipment. As with any historical village, this is best to tour as a pre-arranged group. Docents' insights and stories really help bring the cabins to life.

TY COBB MUSEUM

461 Cook Street (15 miles fro I-85)

Royston 30662

- Phone: (706) 245-1825, **Web: www.tycobbmuseum.org**
- Hours: Monday-Friday 9:00am-4:00pm, Saturday 10:00am-4:00pm. Closed all major holidays.
- Admission: $2.00-$3.00 (age 5+). Military are FREE.

Relive baseball history by viewing artifacts, original works of art and visual accounts of the brilliant player known as "The Georgia Peach." Cobb Theater features stadium-style seating surrounded by a beautiful mural collage. A moving video tribute, narrated by Georgia broadcasting legend Larry Munson, features rare action footage and interviews with Cobb. Cobb's controversial personality earned him the reputation as baseball's fiercest competitor. That zeal carried over to his life outside of baseball, making him a multimillionaire with significant generosity to the community.

VICTORIA BRYANT STATE PARK

1105 Bryant Park Road (I-85 exit 160, 2 miles north of Franklin Springs on GA 327)

Royston 30662

- Phone: (706) 245-6270, **Web: www.gastateparks.org**
- Hours: Daily 7:00am - dark.
- Admission: FREE. Fee for camping.

Nestled in the rolling hills of Georgia's upper piedmont, a beautiful stream flows through the park. Hikers can follow either the short nature trail or the longer perimeter trail that winds through hardwoods and crosses creeks. There is also 8 miles of biking trails, fishing - ponds open to campers and disabled visitors only, and swimming.

HARD LABOR CREEK STATE PARK

P O Box 247 (I-20 exit 105 into town, then 3 miles on Fairplay Road)

Rutledge 30663

- Phone: (706) 557-3001, **Web: www.gastateparks.org**
- Hours: Daily 7:00am-10:00pm.
- Admission: FREE. Camping and cottages and golf extra.

This creek is thought to have been named by slaves who tilled the fields or by Native Americans who found it difficult to work. The park offers a wide range of recreational opportunities in a beautiful wooded setting. Over 24 miles of trails are available for hikers and horseback riders, and a lakeside beach is open for swimming during warmer months. Camping and cottages are available and there are 30 horse stalls, a riding ring and 12 Equestrian Campsites.

SKY VALLEY RESORT

696 Sky Valley Way (US 76 east to US 23 north. Look for signs)

Sky Valley 30537

- Phone: (706) 746-5303, **Web: www.skyvalley.com**

These are Georgia's only ski slopes. Slopes are open mid-December to mid-March. There is NO tubing or sledding on site. Lodge/condos and grounds open year-round. Call for hours and fees.

PANOLA MOUNTAIN STATE CONSERVATION PARK

2600 Highway 155 SW (18 miles southeast of Atlanta on GA 155 via I-20 exit 68), **Stockbridge** 30281

- Phone: (770) 389-7801, **Web: www.gastateparks.org**
- Hours: Daily 7:00am- dark.
- Admission: FREE.
- Tours: Guided 3.5 mile hikes to the mountain are offered Tuesday-Saturday (call for reservations).

This unusual park was created to protect a 100-acre granite monadnock (mountain) often compared to Stone Mountain. Panola Mountain shelters rare plants of the Piedmont region. Hikers may explore the park's watershed and granite outcrop on their own or go on a guided hike onto the restricted-access mountain. The interpretive center has live exhibits, including bees, bats, snakes and turtles. Because of delicate ecological features of the park, pets and bicycles are not allowed on trails.

CHATTAHOOCHEE FOREST NATIONAL FISH HATCHERY

4730 Rock Creek Road (400 North to Dahlonega. Hwy. 60 North to Suches. Continue another 11 miles on Hwy. 60 North. Turn left on Rock Creek Rd), **Suches** 30572

- Phone: (706) 838-4723
  Web: http://southeast.fws.gov/chattahoocheeforest
- Hours: Monday-Friday 7:30am-4:00pm.
- Admission: FREE
- Miscellaneous: U.S. Forest Service campgrounds are located both above and below the hatchery. Family Fish Festival and Kids Day are held annually to promote recreational fishing.

The beautiful surroundings and natural environment draw a lot of visitors to the hatchery. A visitor center, an education center, a visitor kiosk and an opportunity to view the fish in various stages of production draws a crowd. Visitors tour the hatchery annually (call ahead for group tours). Rock Creek, which runs through hatchery property, offers a great trout fishing opportunity. The hatchery annually distributes 324,000 catchable-size rainbow trout to statewide waters allowing thousands of anglers to land a trout.

TRAVELER'S REST STATE HISTORIC SITE

8162 Riverdale Road (six miles east of Toccoa via US 123)

Toccoa 30577

- Phone: (706) 886-2256, **Web: www.gastateparks.org**
- Hours: Thursday-Saturday 9:00am-5:00pm, Sunday 2:00-5:30pm.
- Admission: $1.50-$2.50 per person.

Traveler's Rest was the plantation home of the "richest man in the Tugaloo Valley". To accommodate the growing number of travelers to northeast Georgia, he added on to the structure to house overnight travelers. Today, visitors receive a guided tour of the plantation home with its 90-foot long porch and original antiques, some made by local craftsman, Caleb Shaw.

TOCCOA FALLS

GA Hwy Alt. 17 (from town, take GA Alt 17 one mile)

Toccoa Falls 30598

- Phone: (706) 886-6831 or (800) 868-3257
- Admission: Small admission per person.

On the campus of Toccoa Falls College sits 186-foot high Toccoa Falls, 26 feet higher than Niagara Falls. The Cherokee word "toccoa" means beautiful. From the gift shop and parking area, it is just a short walk along the stream to the base of the falls. A monument reminds visitors of the tragic loss of lives when the earthen dam broke back in the 1970s. The Gate Cottage Restaurant, above the gift shop, has a wonderful buffet on Sundays.

CALLAWAY PLANTATION

US Hwy 78 (US Hwy 78, west of town, across from the Washington-Wilkes Airport)

Washington 30673

- Phone: (706) 678-7060
- Hours: Tuesday-Saturday 10:00am-5:00pm, Sunday 2:00-5:00pm. Closed on thanksgiving, Christmas and New Years.
- Admission: $1.00-$4.00 per person.

Step back in time at Callaway Plantation, a living history museum. The Plantation consists of three restored homes as well as the fields of the farm. The main house (1869) with Greek Revival columns, was the center piece of a 3,000 acre plantation. Virtually unaltered since that time, the home is furnished by period pieces. The oldest building is a hewn log cabin and is believed to have been the home of an early settler. It is a single room cabin with a fireplace for cooking and heating. There is also a 2 story home typical of the 1890 period and an one-room schoolhouse. The entire family will enjoy picking cotton, touring the plantation houses, and seeing primitive crafts.

ROBERT TOOMBS HOUSE STATE HISTORIC SITE

216 E. Robert Toombs Avenue

Washington 30673

- Phone: (706) 678-2226, **Web: www.gastateparks.org**
- Hours: Tuesday-Saturday 9:00am-5:00pm, Sunday 2:00-5:00pm. Closed Monday (except holidays).
- Admission: $1.50-$3.00 per person.

Robert Toombs was a successful planter and lawyer who lead a whirlwind career as a state legislator, US Congressman and Senator. "Defend yourselves, the enemy is at your door…!" thundered Toombs from the Senate floor in January, 1860. The following year, Georgia seceded from the Union and Toombs personified the South by evolving from conservative Unionist to fire-breathing secessionist. Ten years later, as the Reconstruction Era drew to a close in Georgia, Toombs felt that Georgia should live under their own constitution. It was not amended until 65 years later. Visitors can tour the house and grounds, view exhibits and watch a dramatic film portraying an elderly Toombs relating his story to a young reporter.

FORT YARGO STATE PARK

P O Box 764 (1 miles south of Winder on GA 81)

Winder 30680

- Phone: (770) 867-3489, **Web: www.gastateparks.org**
- Hours: Daily 7:00am-10:00pm.
- Admission: FREE. Fee for camping and group shelters.

This historical park features a log fort built in 1792 by settlers for protection against Creek and Cherokee Indians. Fort Yargo offers great camping, hiking and biking (5 miles of trails) and fishing for families. There is also a 260-acre lake with a swimming beach, fishing areas and boat ramps. Many campsites are near the water's edge, and hiking/biking trails follow the lake shore. The park also has pedal boat rentals and miniature golf.

SUGGESTED LODGING AND DINING

LAKE LANIER RESORT - The New England-style LakeHouses On Lanier are nestled among towering Georgia pines on a private, gated peninsula. (770) 945-8787 or **www.lakelanierislands.com**. Rates begin around $175.00 per night for lake houses, near $100.00 per night for hotel rooms. Weekday, AAA and Family Fun discounted rates, too. Just steps away from the waters of Lake Sidney Lanier, these quaint, waterfront villas offer much more than a "traditional" lake house. Equipped with all the conveniences of home but complemented with "creature comforts," including two spacious bedrooms and baths, a great room with a fieldstone fireplace, and a modern kitchen. Each cottage has a deck and full kitchen (except oven). Settle into overstuffed chairs with a good book, relax in the spa (on the deck), throw a steak on the grill or take a walk. Cozy rooms inspire memorable family time!

Chapter 4

North West Area - (NW)

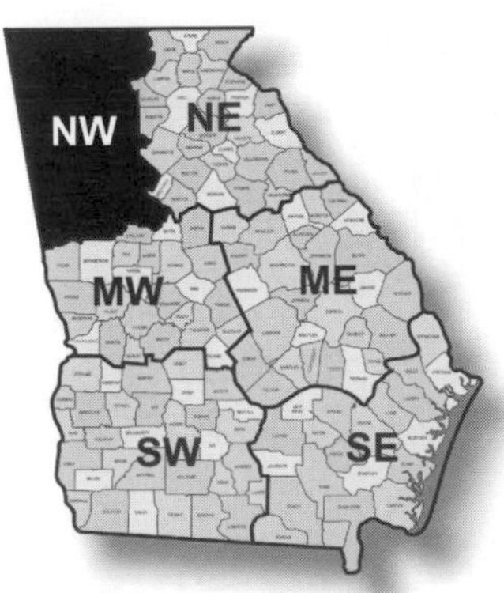

Our Favorites...

* Atlanta Botanical Gardens - Atlanta
* Center for Puppetry - Atlanta
* Margaret Mitchell House/Museum - Atlanta
* Turner Field Tours - Atlanta
* World of Coca Cola - Atlanta
* New Echota Cherokee Capital - Calhoun
* Booth Western Art Museum - Cartersville
* Stone Mountain Park - Stone Mountain

Kid-Friendly Bugs!
Atlanta Botanical Gardens

AMERICAN ADVENTURES PARK

250 Cobb Parkway, North (off I-75 north, Cobb Parkway exit)

Atlanta 30062

- Phone: (770) 424-9283, **Web: www.whitewaterpark.com**
- Hours: Daily (Memorial Day weekend to early August). Weekends only (March-May and August-October). Park usually closes around 7:00pm.
- Admission: $5.00 tickets or $15.00 day pass.

American Adventures, located right next door to Six Flags White Water, is Georgia's only amusement park created especially for families with kids up to the age of 12. It features outdoor amusement rides such as a tilt-a-whirl, scrambler, super slide, miniature roller coaster, balloons, bumper cars and swings suitable for kids up to age 12 (and adults!), plus smaller-scale rides for tots such as trains, planes, teacup twirl, and miniature Ferris wheel. There's also a go-kart race track with two-seat race cars, and 18-hole miniature golf. And in the center of it all is the indoor Foam Factory. The Foam Factory is a multi-level family fun house, featuring foam balls that are catapulted from more than 80 different launchers and blasters strategically placed on three-story towers. Targets, turrets, and baskets can be filled and emptied onto people below, with giant tower-topping baskets that tip over the entire area every few minutes.

APEX MUSEUM

135 Auburn Avenue NE (I-20 East or West to 75/85 North, take Exit # 248B at Edgewood Avenue)

Atlanta 30303

- Phone: (404) 521-2739, **Web: www.apexmuseum.org**
- Hours: Tuesday-Saturday 10:00am-5:00pm, Sunday 1:00-5:00pm. Sundays (February, summer)
- Admission: $3.00-$4.00 (age 4+).

Apex Museum *(cont.)*

The African American Panoramic Experience offers a variety of permanent and temporary exhibits ranging from art to politics. Visit the Yates and Milton Drug Store, one of Atlanta's first Black owned businesses. Hear the stories of early African American pioneers in Atlanta. Learn about the powerful Black Families that helped to make Atlanta great. All Aboard! The Trolley Theater provides the right atmosphere for video presentations on African American experiences. Videos shown are; "Sweet Auburn: Street of Pride", "The Journey", and a number of children's shows (The Croations presentation of inventor Lewis Latimer) & (African Tales of courage, honesty and respect).

PHILIPS EXPERIENCE

One Philips Drive

Atlanta 30303

- Phone: (404) 878-3000 or (800) 326-4000
  Web: www.philipsarena.com
- Hours: During arena games.
- Admission: included with event ticket price.

Within this state of the art multi-purpose sports and entertainment complex (home to the NHL Thrashers and NBA Hawks) there is tons of Philips technology. The Philips Experience is the first interactive space of its kind offering hands-on activities where visitors see, touch, move and control much of the action. Located in the Thrashers Nest some activities include Interactive Alley and Ready, Set, Shoot. While visitors dribble and shoot, specially placed cameras capture their moves from 360 degrees and project it onto screens surrounding the exhibit. This station lets the athlete in everyone shine through for all to see. Shot on

Goal; Screen Test; and Digital Dream Set feature an interactive entertainment system designed to replicate the fun of shooting in true game situations. Or, take a photo celebrity shot and email it to friends. Fans can also keep tabs on the games by watching one of the over 600 Philips TVs throughout the arena.

WORLD OF COCA-COLA

55 Martin Luther King Jr. Drive (adjacent to Underground Atlanta, downtown, exit 248 off I-85/75) Note: Moving to Olympic Park Area, downtown exit International Blvd., **Atlanta** 30303

- Phone: (404) 676-5151 or (800) 676-COKE
  Web: www.woccatlanta.com
- Hours: Monday-Saturday 9:00am-5:00pm. Sunday 11:00am-5:00pm. Closed Easter, Thanksgiving, Christmas and early New Years.
- Admission: $8.00 adult, $7.00 senior (60+), $5.00 child (4-11)
- Miscellaneous: Movies to view on each floor. Photo ops on every floor, too. Giant Coke gift shop.

Atlanta is the birthplace of Coca-Cola. The story is told through a bright collection of memorabilia, classic radio and television ads, a fantasy representation of the bottling process and a futuristic soda fountain. It started with a syrup created by a pharmacist. Accidentally, a soda jerk added carbonated water and the customers loved it - Coke was born! Did you know the secret formula is still a secret? Where is it kept? Did you know a Soda Jerk is called that because they served the soda with a jerk. Take the time to chat with a live soda jerk and you'll be entertained and amused by his thoughts about everything (and anything). The highlight of your visit is the last station - taste testing! Try flavors, old and new, plus many found in foreign countries. Some are quite unusual, some very sweet. If you try them all, like we did, you're bound to have a belly-ache - so, be wise, and choose carefully.

ATLANTA HISTORY CENTER

130 West Paces Ferry Rd, NW (I-75 to exit #255, follow signs 2.5 m)

Atlanta 30305

- Phone: (404) 814-4004, **www.atlantahistorycenter.com**
- Hours: Monday-Saturday 10:00am-5:30pm, Sunday Noon-5:30pm. Closed most holidays.
- Admission: $12.00 adult, $10.00 senior (65+) and student (13+), $7.00 youth (4-12).
- Miscellaneous: Lots of little theatre rooms with videos here. Ask for the Family Fun brochure. Take a walk outside to visit the Swan House 1928 Mansion or the Tullie Smith Farm. The farmhouse and other related buildings are from the 1840s and are best visited during special event programs. Gift shop and Coca-cola Café.

Revisit the Civil War, discover southern folk arts and meet famous Atlantans.

METROPOLITAN FRONTIERS (1835-present): Journey through four stages of Atlanta history, from early pioneer settlements to today's bustling city of international fame. See an entire 1894 shotgun house (why called that? Hint: long, narrow shape) moved from southwest Atlanta; an 1898 horse-drawn fire engine with a steam-driven pump used by the Atlanta fire department in the city's tragic 1917 fire; a 1920 Hanson car built in Atlanta and one of only two known in existence; a scale model of the "Spaghetti Junction".

TURNING POINT: THE AMERICAN CIVIL WAR - Explore the stories of both Confederate and Federal soldiers, along with the heartache and hope of loved ones at home. Videos interpret what happened and why. Touch-screen computer learning stations can answer your questions and deepen your understanding. Did you know only 6% of slaves from Africa went to the States? Others went to the Caribbean and South America.

SHAPING TRADITIONS: FOLK ARTS IN A CHANGING SOUTH - Touch, see, and hear the folk arts that have defined the South for generations. It begins with sections asking "What's folk about folk arts?" and "What's southern about southern folk arts?" Other Exhibits explore: Barbeque, Rednecks, Bobby Jones, and Native American history.

DAD'S GARAGE THEATRE COMPANY

280 Elizabeth Street, Suite C-101

Atlanta 30307

- Phone: (404) 523-3141, **Web: www.dadsgarage.com**

Each week the main character faces an evolving challcngc with a series of special guest characters. In the tradition of youth programmıng at Dad's, this one's for kids and adults alike. Saturday matinees at 1:00pm. $3.00-$5.00 for kids shows.

FERNBANK MUSEUM OF NATURAL HISTORY

767 Clifton Road NE (I-75/I-85/GA400 to downtown exit 248C (GA 10 east). Go 1.7 miles to Ponce de Leon Ave., turn right. Go 1/7 miles to left on Clifton Rd. Follow signs)

Atlanta 30307

- Phone: (404) 929-6300, **Web: www.fernbank.edu/museum**
- Hours: Monday-Saturday 10:00am-5:00pm, Sunday Noon-5:00pm. Only closed Thanksgiving and Christmas.
- Admission: $12.00 adult, $11.00 senior and student, $10.00 child (3-12). IMAX extra $8.00-$10.00. Museum and IMAX combo pricing.
- Miscellaneous: IMAX Theatre shows each day. View schedule and features online. You can also stimulate your senses with lasers, mirrors, water, acoustics and more in Sensing Nature or walk through a World of Shells.

Fernbank Museum Of Natural History *(cont.)*

Giants of the Mesozoic features the world's largest dinosaurs. This area recreates a snapshot of what life was like years ago during the Cretaceous Period. The exhibit showcases the world's largest meat eater, the 47-foot-long Giganotosaurus as it prepares to make a meal out of the largest dinosaur ever discovered, the 123-foot-long plant-eating Argentinosaurus. Also featured in the exhibition are two species of flying reptiles. Twenty-four in all, the pterosaurs are shown reacting to the scene below. The terrain-like rockwork includes fossils of other animals and plants such as a prehistoric frog, crocodile and Auracaria tree, along with dinosaur tracks. A Walk Through Time in Georgia, tells the two-fold story of Georgia's natural history and the development of our planet. Gobs of exhibits and realistic dioramas take you on a journey that begins in the Piedmont, the region in Georgia with the oldest rocks. Then walk in the sand through a marsh or in the muddy swamp. Other highlights include the Cosmos Theatre, a six-foot sloth that lived during the Ice Age, and the Dinosaur Gallery.

FERNBANK SCIENCE CENTER

156 Heaton Park Drive NE (I-285 to exit 39A Decatur/Highway 78)

Atlanta 30307

- Phone: (678) 874-7102, **Web: http://fsc.fernbank.edu**
- Hours: Museum: Monday-Friday 8:30am-5:00pm, Saturday 10:00am-5:00pm, Sunday 1:00-5:00pm. Open until 10:00pm Thursday and Friday. Planetarium: General Times for Family Shows
- Saturday & Sunday 1:30pm. Additional family shows during the summer and some holidays Tuesday-Friday at 11:00am and 1:30pm.
- Admission: Museum is FREE. $3.00-$4.00/planetarium shows.

This learning center has a 500-seat planetarium, an observatory, two electron microscopes, a distance learning studio, a NASA Aeronautics Education lab, and a 65-acre forest. Plan a group or school visit to get the benefit of guided programs - inside and outside.

ATLANTA BOTANICAL GARDEN

1345 Piedmont Avenue (I75/85 exit 14th St., left on Piedmont Ave. at The Prado, Midtown)

Atlanta 30309

- Phone: (404) 876-5859
  Web: www.atlantabotanicalgarden.org
- Hours: Tuesday - Sunday 9:00am-5:00pm, open until 7:00pm during Daylight Savings Time.
- Admission: $12.00 adult, $9.00 senior, $7.00 child (3 and older).
- Miscellaneous: Tropical, desert and endangered plants from around the world are found at Fuqua Conservatory (on the other side of the park).

The Children's Garden, alone, is worth the visit here! Greeted by the "Green Man Fountain and "Plants Keep Us Well" atrium, you'll walk into a garden wonderland where plants help us LAUGH, LIVE AND LEARN. Walk through a cocoon tunnel and emerge as a butterfly. Slide through a leaf, sit around storytime readings of Peter Rabbit, then walk through the story's scenery. Dig for plant fossils, sit in an Indian hut, go to Grandma's House for a visit, play the bee game, and climb in a giant tree house. This is, by far, the best children's garden we've interacted with in the South!

ATLANTA SYMPHONY ORCHESTRA

1280 Peachtree Street N.E. (Atlanta Symphony Hall, Woodruff Arts Center. Take I-75 South to Exit 250 (10th Street/14 Street), turn left to Peachtree), **Atlanta** 30309

- Phone: (404) 733-5000, (404) 733-4900
  Web: www.atlantasymphony.org

Family Concert: Introduce your youngest family members to the fun world of symphonic music as dancers, puppeteers and your favorite storybook characters join the orchestra. Pre-concert cookies and juice are provided. Concerts are Sundays at 1:30 & 3:30 pm. Musical Storytime: Series incorporates Family Concert themes into wonderfully interactive, fun storytimes at 4 metro Atlanta Borders stores. Call (404) 733-4734 for more information. Each year the Youth Orchestra performs at least three subscription concerts.

CENTER FOR PUPPETRY ARTS

1404 Spring Street, NW (I75 Exit #250 (10th/14th/GA Tech). Turn left on 14th Street, crossing over I-75. At 3rd traffic light, turn left on W. Peachtree Street), **Atlanta** 30309

- Phone: (404) 873-3391, **Web: www.puppet.org**
- Hours: Tuesday-Saturday 9:00am-5:00pm, Sunday 11:00am-5:00pm. Open until showtime for evening performances.
- Admission: $12.00 per person per performance. Workshop and Museum admission included in single show ticket.
- Miscellaneous: Museum and performances change throughout the year. Excellent Education programs and study guides. Reservations suggested for activities. Take a special Behind-The-Scenes Tour at the Center for Puppetry Arts and get a peek at how puppet magic is made (weekends at 2:00pm for groups - $5.00 extra).

Many famous puppets have spent the night here (how about Kermit the Frog). Can you imagine the stories this place could tell? So, let's start in the Museum. First of all, it's a little spooky and interactive (even the storage room is animated). The best part - the variety. Asians spend their lifetimes perfecting Shadow puppets and Bunraku puppetry requires three puppeteers to work one figure. Other puppets are much simpler. Kid's imaginations soar seeing household objects like scarves, cloth, and plastic tubing puppets. Now, attend a performance. Their shows are really several notches above any puppet shows elsewhere. Many are based on classic folk tales - some with a "twist". You are encouraged to laugh, giggle, sneer, clap or stomp approval or disapproval at the happenings on stage. The puppeteers greet the audience afterwards to enlighten the crowd and share their "tricks". Next, do a workshop. Learn about different types of puppets - hand, rod, string, marionette, shadow or body. Make your own hand puppet that resembles a character in the performance. Have a short time to perform with your puppet in the mini-stage. What a wonderful way to engage the kids into the art and entertainment of puppetry. This place is a wonderful surprise every visit and worth spending a good part of your morning / afternoon!

FEDERAL RESERVE BANK OF ATLANTA VISITORS CENTER & MONETARY MUSEUM

1000 Peachtree Street NE

Atlanta 30309

- Phone: (404) 498-8764
  www.frbatlanta.org/atlantafed/visitors_center/vc_index.cfm
- Admission: FREE
- Tours: Open for scheduled, guided tours only weekdays at 10:00am or 1:00pm. Recommended for pre-teens on up.

Federal Reserve Bank of Atlanta Visitors Center & Monetary Museum *(cont.)*

The story of money—from bartering to modern times. In the museum, you'll see examples of rare coins and currency plus displays highlighting noted events in monetary history. After touring the museum, experience the rest of the Visitors Center, where interactive and multimedia exhibits provide in-depth lessons on the role of the Federal Reserve in the U.S. economy. Then, you can take a look inside their cash-processing operations, where millions of dollars are counted, sorted, or shredded daily. You'll also get a glimpse into the bank's automated vault and see the robotic transports that do the heavy lifting.

HIGH MUSEUM OF ART

1280 Peachtree Street, **Atlanta** 30309

- Phone: (404) 733-4400, **Web: www.high.org**
- Hours: Tuesday-Saturday 10:00am-5:00pm, Sunday Noon-5:00pm.
- Admission: $8.00 adult, $6.00 senior, $4.00 child (6-17).
- Tours: Guided tours Sunday and Wednesday at 1:00pm.

This museum mostly displays European and American paintings and special exhibits including African, decorative, folk and modern art. The Learning to Look / Looking to Learn interactives are the best way to explore a classic art museum with kids.

MARGARET MITCHELL HOUSE & MUSEUM

990 Peachtree Street (I-75, 10th Street exit and Peachtree)

Atlanta 30309

- Phone: (404) 249-7015, **Web: www.gwtw.org**
- Hours: Open daily 9:30am-5:00pm.

- Admission: $12.00 adult, $8.00 senior (65+) and students over 18, $5.00 youth (6-17).
- Miscellaneous: Because Margaret was quite a character, ask for the family-friendly version of the apartment tour.

Tour the historic house and apartment where Margaret Mitchell wrote one of the classic beloved novels "Gone With the Wind". As you learn about the life (and death) of this fascinating woman you'll learn that she wrote short stories as a little girl - she even put on plays with neighboring children. The girls were always the heroine! Her Dad was a history buff and many characters are based on family and friends throughout Margaret's life history. In the "Gone With the Wind" movie museum, your girls will love to admire the doll collection and everyone will want to "walk thru" the actual doorway to "Tara"! Now, prepare, girls and boys, to be inspired! Touch her lucky stair post or see her battered typewriter where she wrote most of her work. When friends came over, she'd hide her manuscript all over the house. She oncc forgot the first chapter was hidden in the refrigerator! Amusing stories abound while on tour. We promise, you'll be told a secret or two!

NATIONAL MUSEUM OF PATRIOTISM

1405 Spring Street NW (located about 2.5 blocks from the Arts Center, I-75 exit 103)

Atlanta 30309

- Phone: (404) 875-0691 or (877) 276-1692
  Web: www.museumofpatriotism.org
- Hours: Saturday, Sunday, Tuesday, Wednesday, Thursday 10:00am to 4:00pm.
- Admission: $6.00 adult, $4.00 senior (65+)/ Student (age 7+), FREE - Active Duty Military.

Complete with visual aids and interactivity, this museum helps school children and families connect with the founders of our country and understand the values that have created the greatest nation on earth. Begin your tour as the Immigrant Experience focuses on the "melting pot" of diverse cultures and the opportunities offered to immigrants of yesterday. Learn how immigrants are giving back to our country today. In the Hall of Patriots ordinary people who have done extra-ordinary things in the name of country are honored. Here you can understand that anyone can be a patriot. The Olympic Games represent the single largest volunteer endeavor in the world. The display shows how volunteering one's spirit and enthusiasm can inspire greatness in all. Finally, the Sweetheart Jewelry display showcases the largest collection of wartime jewelry made and sold. Loved ones who sent their boys to war will fondly remember these and probably want to share a story or two with you. Experiencing the words and deeds of our heroes - both ordinary and extra-ordinary - will inspire your patriotism.

MARTIN LUTHER KING JR. NATIONAL HISTORIC SITE

450 Auburn Avenue, N.E. (I-75 exit 248D)

Atlanta 30312

- Phone: (404) 331-6922, **Web: www.nps.gov/malu**
- Hours: Daily 10:00am-5:00pm. Summers open until 6:00pm.The Home and Church may have shorter hours, please inquire at the Park Service desk for tour times.
- Admission: FREE

Now, a National Historic Site, visit Dr. Martin Luther King Jr.'s Birthplace, Home and Church. Begin in the Visitor Center for orientation. The "Civil Rights Struggle" present emotional exhibits through movie and video clips. Most exhibits encourage children to carry on the dream of freedom, justice and world peace using interactive displays. The exhibits are extremely emotional and capture your attention and your heart. However, it may contain material that is best viewed by children who have studied segregation and Civil Rights beforehand. Otherwise, your children may be terrified how cruel people can be to one another. The Home is located in the residential section of "Sweet Auburn", the center of black Atlanta. Two blocks west of the home is Ebenezer Baptist Church, the pastorate of Martin's grandfather and father. The tour guide at the church "preaches" the church's history from near the pulpit! Here, "M.L." learned about family and Christian love, segregation in the days of "Jim Crow" laws, diligence and tolerance.

ATLANTA FALCONS

One Georgia Dome Drive

Atlanta 30313

- Phone: (404) 249-6400 or (800) 326-4000
  Web: www.atlantafalcons.com

NFL Atlanta Falcons play each autumn and winter football season with an average of 10 games at home. Meet the mascot Freddie Falcon at most games. Falcons Landing will once again be open to the public 3 hours prior to kick-off for all Falcon home games. At each home game, Falcons Landing will feature a different band, live on the Coca-Cola stage. Children and adults alike will enjoy participating in a variety of free activities. Practice kicking field goals, fielding punts, or testing your quarterbacking skills on the gridiron. Check out Falcons central where you can have your face painted while listening to local radio stations broadcasting their pre-game shows live from the landing.

CENTENNIAL OLYMPIC PARK

285 International Blvd., **Atlanta** 30313

- Phone: (404) 223-4412, **Web: www.centennialpark.com**
- Hours: Daily 7:00am-11:00pm.
- Admission: FREE

Look for the Fountain of Rings - the world's largest fountain utilizing the five interconnecting rings of the Olympic symbol with 25 water jets - and you've found the park. The water jets display four 20-minute musical water shows daily beginning at lunchtime, then every three hours. There are also playgrounds, water gardens, a visitors center with Fountainside Cafe, and people-watchers plaza.

CHILDREN'S MUSEUM OF ATLANTA, IMAGINE IT!

275 Centennial Olympic Park Drive NW (south on I-75/85 exit Williams Street. Turn right onto Baker Street)

Atlanta 30313

- Phone: (404) 659-5437, **Web: www.imagineit-cma.org**
- Hours: Monday-Saturday 10:00am-5:00pm, Sunday Noon-5:00pm. Closed Mondays during the school year and closed one hour early on weekdays. Closed major holidays.
- Admission: $11.00 per person age 3 to adult.

Kids and their adults can learn together where food comes from (and how the body uses it), work construction equipment, explore a barnyard, and make a craft to take home. You can even walk through a make-believe town and go shopping. The museum is ideal for children age 8 and younger.

GEORGIA DOME TOURS

One Georgia Dome NW (tours depart between Gates B & C)

Atlanta 30313

- Phone: (404) 223-8600, **Web: www.gadome.com**
- Admission: $6.00 adult, $4.00 senior and child (5-12).
- Tours: Individual Tours: Tuesday-Saturday 10:00am-3:00pm during football season (except on days when events occur in the Dome). Tours leave every hour.

The world's largest cable-supported dome offers tours. Want to see behind-the-scenes, from the Falcons locker room, to the new turf everyone is talking about? Want to see the VIP views from the press box or Dome suites? Come see the site of the 1994 & 2000 Super Bowls. Visit the venue that hosted gymnastics & basketball for the 1996 Summer Olympics.

ATLANTA BRAVES

755 Hank Aaron Drive (Turner Field, just southeast of downtown)

Atlanta 30315

- Phone: (404) 249-6400 or (800) 326-4000
  Web: http://atlanta.braves.mlb.com

Major League Baseball team plays regular season March through September. Tickets range $1.00 (Clark Howard Skyline seats) to $45 (dugout). Turner Field combines the nostalgia and the atmosphere of old-time baseball with a state-of-the-art environment unlike any other park. To keep the kids busy during the game try: Getting your face airbrushed at the Braves free Fun Zone; testing your baseball skills in Scouts Alley; or, bang the over-sized Braves drum. Kids 14 and under are invited to join the NEW Atlanta Braves Kids Club. Your one-year membership is FREE and includes great gifts and discounts. Plus, learn about opportunities to meet and greet with the team mascot, Homer the baseball. Kids, run the bases after the game on Sundays.

ATLANTA CYCLORAMA

800 Cherokee Ave. SE (I-20 to exit 59a (Boulevard). Follow signs. The Cyclorama is located next to Zoo Atlanta in Grant Park)

Atlanta 30315

- Phone: (404) 658-7625
  Web: www.webguide.com/cyclorama.html
- Hours: Daily 9:20am-4:30pm.
- Admission: $7.00 adult, $6.00 senior (60+), $5.00 child (6-12)

Home of the world's largest painting, "The Battle of Atlanta". Through spectacular music, art and sound effects, history comes alive as you step back to July 22, 1864 and become part of the eight hour battle. Cycloramas place the spectator in the middle (standing or sitting) as you "follow" the sequence of events. Shows begin with a film that covers the history of the Atlanta Campaign leading up to the battle narrated by James Earl Jones. Tiered central seating is lit as you enter, then the house lights dim. Each section of the painting is viewed from the slowly rotating seating and a guide points out highlights of the painting. Look for General Sherman and Old Abe (the eagle). After the show you may visit a Civil War museum that includes The Texas, a Civil War era train that was engaged in an episode now commonly called "The Great Locomotive Chase."

BRAVES MUSEUM & HALL OF FAME/TURNER FIELD TOURS

755 Hank Aaron Drive (I-75/85 exit 246, Fulton Street East)

Atlanta 30315

- Phone: (404) 614-2310, **Web: http://atlanta.braves.mlb.com**
- Hours: The museum opens two and a half hours before each game and closes in the middle of the seventh inning.
- Admission: Museum Only: $2.00-$5.00. Tour/Museum: $10.00 adult, $5.00 child. FREE parking in the Green Lot.

- Tours: On non-game days, tours are offered Monday - Saturday from 9:00am - 3:00pm and Sundays from 1:00-3:00pm. On game-days, tours are offered Monday - Saturday from 9:00am - noon. Please note that there are no tours offered before any afternoon or Sunday home game. Tours start at the top of each hour and last approximately one hour. No reservations are necessary.

The museum is the starting point of Turner Field Tours and traces the Braves History. The museum features memorabilia commemorating legends of the game and key moments in Braves history from Boston to Milwaukee to Atlanta. The museum displays artifacts including Hank Aaron's historic 715th home run bat and ball, more than 50 game jerseys, game bats, an actual railroad car from the B&O Railroad used to transport players in the 1950s, the knee brace worn by Sid Bream during his famous slide into home plate that captured the 1992 NLCS pennant for the Braves, and the 1995 World Series trophy and championship rings. The Tour is probably the highlight of the visit. See Sky Field, a luxury suite, the press box & broadcast booth, the dugout, and the Plaza with the giant baseballs. But the real behind-the-scenes fun is a peek in the locker room. Look for the "putting green" and the 561 TVs throughout the stadium. They have more TVs here than trash cans! What young, little leaguer wouldn't love this tour?

ZOO ATLANTA

800 Cherokee Avenue SE, **Atlanta** 30315

- Phone: (404) 624-5822, **Web: www.zooatlanta.org**
- Hours: Daily 9:30am-4:30pm (5:30pm on weekends). Grounds remain open 1 hour after admissions close. Closed on Thanksgiving, Christmas & New Year's Day.
- Admission: $17.00 adult, $13.00 senior (55+), $12.00 child (3-11).

Zoo Atlanta *(cont.)*

Don't miss the Giant Pandas of Chengdu (what are their favorite scents? What do they like to eat?)! See gorillas, orangutans, tigers, lions, giraffes, elephants, birds & more in natural habitats. See more than 700 animals representing 200 species from all over the world.

AMERICAN MUSEUM OF PAPERMAKING

500 Tenth Street N.W. (IPST Bldg. At Georgia Tech)

Atlanta 30332

- Phone: (404) 894-7840, **Web: www.ipst.edu/amp**
- Hours: Monday-Friday 9:00am-5:00pm.
- Admission: FREE. Suggested donation $3.00 per person.
- Tours: By Reservation. Grades 3-12. Minimum 10, Maximum 30-40. Fee for tours (see below)

Trace the history of paper from 4,000 BC to today. Learn how Asians started a fine art and how companies through the ages each developed a way to "watermark" their signature on their product. The gallery showcases the work of contemporary paper artists. The American Museum of Papermaking offers two guided tours:

THE PAPER ROAD - Follow the path of papermaking that began in ancient China and leads to the advanced technology of today. This tour includes a guided tour of the Museum of Papermaking as well as "Paper-The Video", a fun and lively video which highlights the history and the uses of paper. The charge for this tour is $5.00 per person. Tuesday-Friday 10:00am. Allow 1 hour.

PAPERWORKS! - This includes a guided tour of the Museum of Papermaking and "Paper-The Video", as well as a hands-on papermaking workshop. Students will enjoy making their own sheets of paper from cotton pulp. The charge for this tour is $7.00 per person. Tuesday-Friday 10:00am. Allow 1½ hours.

GEORGIA STATE CAPITOL & MUSEUM

Capitol Hill at Washington Street (look for the gold domed building)

Atlanta 30334

- Phone: (404) 656-2844, **Web: www.sos.state.ga.us/museum**
- Hours: Monday-Friday 8:00am-5:00pm.
- Admission: FREE

Native Georgia gold tops the dome of this state capital, an 1889 building that houses a Hall of Flags, Hall of Fame, and a natural science museum. The fourth floor is where you'll spend most of your time on this self-guided tour. Here, you'll be able to peek in the gallery overlooking the Senate and House Chambers - they look serious, don't they? This floor is also host to many displays of the history of Georgia. We learned cotton used to be the cash crop here. When it faded, what three "P's" took over? - peaches, pecans and peanuts.

CNN STUDIO TOUR

One CNN Center (I-75/85 exit International Blvd., left on Olympic Park)

Atlanta 30348

- Phone: (404) 827-2300 or (877) 4CNN-Tour
  Web: www.cnn.com/studiotour
- Admission: $10.00 adult, $8.00 senior (65+), $7.00 child (4-12). Must be at least 4 years old.
- Tours: Daily from 9:00am - 5:00pm. Tours depart every 10 minutes from Atrium. Tours last 50 minutes. Advance reservations suggested.

This attraction showcases the CNN Studios. On tour, get a look inside the CNN production studios and newsrooms. Begin by looking at 30+ monitors simulating the CNN control Room. A one-of-a-kind re-creation of CNN's main control room where guests will see and hear the truly behind-the-scenes elements of 24-hour news, live. Look for the monitor with the pre-shot - maybe catch an anchor powdering their nose! An interactive exhibit area follows. This is where guests can view video clips of the top 100 news stories that CNN has covered during the past 20 years, log on to CNN.com, and test their knowledge with the journalism ethics display. Next, see a sample studio - be sure to volunteer to do a short broadcast. Why can't weather people wear blue? Check out the robotic cameras. The Tour Finale features a special presentation showcasing the networks that make up the rest of the Turner Broadcasting family such as TBS, TNT, and the Cartoon Network. Great tour to see the glamour and electronic glitz it takes to pull off a 24-hour broadcast.

CHATTAHOOCHEE RIVER NATIONAL RECREATION AREA

1978 Island Ford Parkway (GA 400 exit 6, onto Dunwoody Place. Go 0.5 miles to Roberts Drive, turn right and go about a mile)

Atlanta 30350

- Phone: (770) 399-8070, **Web: www.nps.gov/chat**
- Hours: Island Ford Visitor Center 9:00am-5:00pm daily. Park is open from dawn to dark all year long.
- Admission: $2.00 per day per vehicle.

Take a solitary walk to enjoy nature's display, raft leisurely through the rocky shoals with friends, fish the misty waters, or hike and picnic along the trails.

SIX FLAGS OVER GEORGIA AMUSEMENT PARK

275 Riverside Pkwy.

Atlanta (Austell) 30168

- Phone: (770) 948-9290
  Web: www.sixflags.com/parks/overgeorgia/index.asp
- Hours: Daily (late May through mid-August). Weekends (April-May, late August-October).
- Admission: $43.99 regular, $25.99 senior and child (under 48" tall). Season passes & online discounts are worth the effort.

This is a premier family theme park. Six Flags Over Georgia continues to make significant additions to its family offerings, including five new rides (just last year) that parents and kids can enjoy together. Last summer Six Flags Over Georgia unveiled its tenth roller coaster, Wile E. Coyote Canyon Blaster based on the Warner Bros. Looney Tunes character, Wile E. Coyote. Step inside the Drive-In Theatre for the park's hottest new show, TOTALLY POP! Superman-Ultimate Flight, another newer ride, joins the numerous other roller coasters, thrill rides and entertainment.

DUNWOODY NATURE CENTER

5343 Roberts Drive (Rte. 400 north to exit 6)

Atlanta (Dunwoody) 30338

- Phone: (740) 394-3322, **Web: www.dunwoodynature.org**
- Hours: Park is open sun-up to sundown, daily. Nature Center is open Monday-Friday 9:00am-5:00pm, and Saturdays by event.
- Admission: FREE. Programs and I-SPY rentals ($10.00) carry a fee.

Dunwoody Nature Center *(cont.)*

- Miscellaneous: Sign up to rent one of their I-SPY Packs and lead your own exploration through the park, any day of the week. Self-guided activities, games, learning tools and more will engage Pre-K through High School students in outdoor learning. Homeschool families, who seek activities for a wide age-range, will appreciate the variety of resources in each pack.

The Park features wetland, two miles of woodland and streamside trails; display gardens; a picnic meadow; and a shaded playground. The Boardwalk meanders through part of the park and is where you'll learn about the great diversity of plant and animal life in the wetlands without damage to this fragile but hard-working ecosystem. You can even do all of this without getting your shoes dirty. The Nature Center includes a Compost Demonstration Site, How Worms Work, a Honeybee Observation Hive (under guidance, kids may even get to handle the Queen), and the Raptor Information Center (Learn about their habitat, food, habits, building nest boxes for owls, and wing span).

GEORGIA BALLET

31 Atlanta Street, third floor (performances at Cobb County Civic Center's Anderson Theatre. I-75 exit 263 west)

Atlanta (Marietta) 30060

- Phone: (770) 425-0258, **Web: www.georgiaballet.org**

This Professional dance company provides a school-year season of many family-oriented ballets. Watch as toymakers or foreign people tell their story through dance. They perform renditions of the famous Nutcracker each year in December.

BIG CHICKEN, THE

US 41 at Roswell Street, **Atlanta (Marietta)** 30062

The Big Chicken is the extraordinary sign for a very ordinary KFC in Marietta. In 1963, the owner of a drive-in wanted to draw attention. And thus, Tubby Davis, owner of Johnny Reb's Restaurant, and an egghead Georgia Tech engineering student built the world's first and only post-modern cubist steel chicken. Using locally milled steel, it stands 50-feet tall. Three decades and several owners later, the Big Chicken still rises proudly above Cobb Parkway. Its legacy has even spread to surrounding businesses, many using the nomenclature of "Big Chicken This"...

WHITE WATER PARK, SIX FLAGS

250 Cobb Parkway, North (off I-75 north

Atlanta (Marietta) 30062

- Phone: (770) 424-WAVE, **Web: www.whitewaterpark.com**
- Hours: Vary from 10:00am-6:00pm pre-season and post-season to 10:00am-8:00pm peak season. Park open weekends in May, daily Memorial Day- mid August, weekends though Labor Day.
- Admission: $20.00-$30.00 day tickets.

The South's largest water theme park with nearly 50 water play fun activities. A variety of thrilling water slides, rides, attractions, and special areas for small children are featured at this water park where you will find "The Ocean," a 750,000 gallon pool that whips up four foot waves and "The Cliffhanger," one of the tallest freefalls in the world where the rider is propelled 90 feet straight down at high-speed. Or, try the 735-foot-long Run-a-Way River, a vicious four-person tunnel raft ride. If that's not enough, try the new "Tornado" (riders are set in motion down a 132-foot long tunnel and thrown into the giant open-ended funnel),

Bermuda Triangle, Gulf Coast Screamer or Banzai Pipeline. For Little Kids (and Chickens): There are other ways to play—splash in Little Squirt's Island and Captain Kid's Cove, or just float down one of two lazy rivers. And everybody loves the 750,000 gallon wavepool, family raft rides and body flumes. For Everyone: The Pirate Invasion Dive Show brings Vegas-show glitz and high-diving heroics to the wavepool most weeknights, followed on summer Fridays by "Dive-In Movies." Float up to the big screen or find a seat on the deck for a family-friendly flick. Never was cinema more refreshing.

BULLOCH HALL

180 Bulloch Avenue (Intersection of GA Hwy 120 and GA Hwy 9. Bulloch Hall is located just one block west of the Historic Square)

Atlanta (Roswell) 30075

- Phone: (770) 992-1731 or (800) 776-7935
  Web: www.bullochhall.org
- Hours: Monday-Saturday 10:00am-3:00pm, Sunday 1:00-3:00pm.
- Admission: $6.00 adult, $4.00 student (6-12).

Mittie Bulloch Roosevelt was a Georgia lady who left a legacy that would impact a nation and the world. Her son, Theodore Roosevelt, served as the 26th President of the United States. Her granddaughter would marry Franklin Roosevelt, serve as our nation's First Lady, and change the role of women in the White House. Mittie's childhood home is open for docent-lead tours including the house, slave quarters, garden and grounds.

CHATTAHOOCHEE NATURE CENTER

9135 Willeo Road (I-285 exit US 19 north. Turn left on Azalea, then left on Willeo)

Atlanta (Roswell) 30075

- Phone: (770) 992-2055, **Web: www.chattnaturecenter.com**
- Hours: Monday -Saturday 9:00am-5:00pm. Sunday Noon-5:00pm.
- Admission: $2.00-$3.00 (age 3+).

An environmental education facility located on the banks of the Chattahoochee River, the Chattahoochee Nature Center is home to a variety of woodland and wetland critters—waterfowl, birds of prey, reptiles. You might even spot a beaver or otter rippling through a pond. Injured owls, hawks, raccoons, and other animals are brought here for rehabilitation and eventual return to the wild. Short interpretative hiking trails, canoe trips and a scenic river boardwalks let you spend as little as an hour or most of the day in the wilds of this natural habitat without really "roughing it." Live animal demonstrations are usually held in the exhibition center, where you can also watch honey bees at work or peek into "life in a log." Among the center's special programs is an overnight camping experience complete with a workshop on nocturnal animals.

SMITH PLANTATION HOME

935 Alpharetta Street,

Atlanta (Roswell) 30075

- Phone: (740) 641-3978
  Web: www.cvb.roswell.ga.us/attractions3b.html
- Admission: $6.00 adult, $4.00 child (6-12).
- Tours: Monday-Friday at 11:30am to 2:30pm. Saturday 10:30am-1:30pm. Tours leave on the half hour. Closed New Years, July 4th, Thanksgiving and Christmas.

Smith Plantation Home *(cont.)*

- Miscellaneous: Try to tour with other families or a school group - the "kids" version tour is best for grade-schoolers.

Guides in period costume invite you to spend 45 minutes to one hour with the memories and artifacts of three generations of the Archibald Smith family. Built in 1845, the Smith's livelihood was cotton crops and they kept around 30 slaves to help with the work. In the main house, you will get a chance to touch cotton plants, figure out how long it took to make a simple turkey sandwich for lunch, see an unusual "fly swatter" centerpiece!, or glance at family pictures (why aren't they smiling?). Outside, you'll peek in working outbuildings - the cook house, a spring house (used as a frig) and a slave cabin.

ANDRETTI SPEED LAB

11000 Alpharetta Highway (I-75 north to Hwy 400 north to exit 8, left on Mansell, right on Hwy 9)

Atlanta (Roswell) 30076

- Phone: (770) 992-5688, **Web: www.andrettispeedlab.com**
- Hours: Monday-Saturday 11:00am-10:00pm, Sunday Noon-10:00pm.
- Admission: Varies, depending on activity.
- Miscellaneous: Fuddruckers Restaurant (with racing theme) on the premises. To race in cars, you must be wearing closed-toe, closed-heel shoes.

Got the need for speed? It's fulfilled and thrilled here! The unique, indoor event center offers rack track driving, rock climbing and one of the largest arcade areas in the southeast (mostly "speed" oriented games and simulators). The Junior Karts (age 8+) are an indoor, high performance, miniature speedway course. Get suited up after you pass your drivers test. The orientation room is where techs (in white lab coats) teach you the basics before you get behind the wheel.

NEW ECHOTA CHEROKEE CAPITAL

1211 Chatsworth Highway NE (one mile east of I-75 exit 317 on GA 225), **Calhoun** 30701

- Phone: (706) 624-1321, **Web: www.gastateparks.org**
- Hours: Tuesday-Saturday 9:00am-5:00pm, Sunday 2;00-5:30pm. Closed Monday (except holidays), Thanksgiving, Christmas and New Years. Closed Tuesday if open Monday.
- Admission: $2.50-$3.50 per person.

The Cherokee National group established New Echota as its capital in 1825. This government seat became headquarters for the independent Indian nation that once covered northern Georgia and parts of four other southeastern states. This is the site of the first Nativc American newspaper office, the signing of a treaty which relinquished Cherokee claims to lands east of the Mississippi, and finally, the sad assembly of Cherokee Indians for the removal along the infamous Trail of Tears. Many artifacts from the original print shop and methods of archeological digs are on display. Today, the site has a museum where you can view a 17-minute video and then take a self-guided tour of historic buildings. The structures include: a print shop, a court house, Council House, a missionary home, Vann's tavern and several homes and farm buildings. Did you know the Cherokee were the most civilized Indian tribe? Learn some Cherokee language with Sequoyah: *si-yo* = Hello, *ga-du* = bread, *a-ma* = water.

CAGLE'S DAIRY FARM

362 Stringer Road (I-75 north to I-575 north. Exit 14 at Holly Springs. Take the right as you come off the ramp at Hickory Road)

Canton 30115

- Phone: (770) 345-5591, **Web: www.caglesdairy.com**
- Admission: $6.00 per person
- Tours: Tour lasts about 1-1/2 hours. They have a grassy area to sit and have a picnic lunch.

Cagle's Dairy Farm *(cont.)*

Children should have the opportunity to learn that their food (including milk) is produced on a farm and is not just a product of the local grocery store. The only dairy in Georgia to milk the cows and put the milk in the jug right on the farm wants groups to visit a real working farm. The Dairy Tour is divided into several stages, starting with a hay ride and herding demonstration by Scott Cagle's award-winning Border Collies. You will see baby calves being bottle fed, and get a first-hand look at how a live cow is milked. You will also visit the Processing Facility. Children will learn how milk gets from the cow to the grocery store. Each tour guest gets a free 1/2 pint of plain or chocolate milk. And they have a grassy spot just right for your blanket and a picnic lunch!

JOHN TANNER STATE PARK

354 Tanner's Beach Road (6 miles west of town off GA 16)

Carrollton 30117

- Phone: (770) 830-2222, **Web: www.gastateparks.org**
- Hours: Daily 7:00am-10:00pm.
- Admission: FREE. Fee for camping and group lodge.

This Georgia park is best known for having the largest sand swimming beach of any Georgia state park. Water lovers find a haven here looking for boating and fishing. Or, enjoy camping, mini-golf, volleyball, pedal boats and horseshoes. The small lodge near the beach has six units, each with fully equipped kitchens, dining area, living area and bedroom. There are two hiking/nature trails - one 1/4 mile and the other 1-mile lake loop trail. Boating is electric motors only.

BARTOW HISTORY CENTER

13 Museum Drive (downtown, follow signs from I-75)

Cartersville 30120

- Phone: (770) 382-3818,
  Web: www.bartowhistorycenter.org
- Hours: Tuesday-Saturday 10:00am-5:00pm, Sunday 1:00-5:00pm, plus Thursday evenings.
- Admission: $2.00-$3.00 (Students and adults).

Exhibits at the Bartow History Center focus on the settlement and development of Bartow County, Georgia, beginning with the early nineteenth century, when the Cherokee still inhabited the area. Pioneer life, Civil War strife, post-war recovery, the Great Depression era, early industry, and notable figures are depicted through interactive exhibits in the permanent gallery space. At the History Center, kids can practice penmanship on slate boards, recite lessons, and perform school chores to avoid wearing the dunce cap. Learn map skills with games and puzzles at the History Center. Sit down at the switchboard and explore the history of communication from tin can phones to old radio shows.

BOOTH WESTERN ART MUSEUM

501 Museum Drive (I-75 exit 288, Main St. Go west 2.2 miles, follow signs), **Cartersville** 30120

- Phone: (770) 387-1300, **Web: www.boothmuseum.org**
- Hours: Tuesday-Saturday 10:00am-5:00pm, Sunday 1:00-5:00pm. Thursday open until 8:00pm.
- Admission: $6.00 adult, $5.00 senior, $4.00 student (over 12)

Explore the West without leaving the South! This place is spectacular! Start with an orientation film about the history of the West. Then, kids receive a saddle bag filled with activity sheets and sample artifacts. This "scavenger hunt" method is very engaging and even has a beaded bracelet kit to take home (the rest of the bag's contents remain for the next child). Now, if that wasn't fun enough, head downstairs to Sagebrush Ranch hands-on area. Begin by dressing up as a cowgirl or boy (chaps and all). Take a ride in the rocking stagecoach, sit on a life-size horse or brand a cow. Draw, ride, cook, puzzle or read, too. It's authentic and it's a hoot! Not many art museums are this kid-friendly anywhere - and, such a fun theme - cowboys and Indians. Excellent!

ETOWAH INDIAN MOUNDS STATE HISTORIC SITE

813 Indian Mounds Road SE (5 miles SW of I-75 exit 288, follow brown directional signs)

Cartersville 30120

- Phone: (770) 387-3747, **Web: www.gastateparks.org**
- Hours: Tuesday-Saturday 9:00am-5:00pm, Sunday 2;00-5:30pm. Closed Monday (except holidays), Thanksgiving, Christmas and New Years. Closed Tuesday when open Monday.
- Admission: $2.00-$3.00 per person.

These mounds were the ceremonial center of a town that was home to several thousand Mississippian Indians more that 400 years ago. All the mounds are flat-topped and made from earthen material (dirt). The largest stands 63 acres and appears to serve as the temple for the "Priest-Chief" and as burial sites for Indian nobility. You actually get to climb the 134 steps to walk along the top. In another mound, nobility were buried in elaborate costumes accompanied by items they would need in their after-lives. Many artifacts in the museum show how the natives of this political and religious center decorated themselves with shell beads, tattoos, paint, feathers and copper earrings. You'll see a sample burial site and fish traps. Well-preserved stone effigies and objects made of wood, sea shells and stone are also displayed. This is a mysterious site because these were prehistoric peoples and no one recorded history. The mounds are very well-preserved and fun (but aerobic) to climb.

RED TOP MOUNTAIN STATE PARK

50 Lodge road (1.5 miles east of I-75 via exit 285)

Cartersville 30121

- Phone: (770) 975-0055 lodge or (770) 975-4226 center
  Web: www.gastateparks.org
- Hours: Daily 7:00am-10:00pm.

Named for the soil's rich red color caused by high iron-ore content, Red Top Mountain was once an important mining area for iron. Now, this park is on Lake Allatoona and is especially ideal for swimming (beach and pool), boating, and fishing. Several hiking trails wind through the park (12 miles of trails, 3/4 paved). The park's lodge and restaurant plus many cottages, offer overnight accommodations. There's also mini-golf and sport courts.

CAVE SPRING AND ROLATER PARK

Cave Spring Square (southwest of Rome, on Hwy 411, South)

Cave Spring 30124

- Phone: (706) 777-0933

Located in shady Rolater Park, just off the town square, are the natural limestone cave and spring which are the town's namesakes. Open to the public, the cave has impressive stalagmites and the legendary "Devil's Stool" formation. The spring water has won awards for purity and taste and is commercially bottled. Many visitors bring jugs to fill at the spring and take home for drinking. A favorite with locals is swimming in the 1.5 acre chlorine-free pool shaped like the state of Georgia. Open daily. FREE.

CHIEF VANN HOUSE STATE HISTORIC SITE

82 GA 225 North (outskirts of town at the intersection of GA 225 and GA 52A)

Chatsworth 30705

- Phone: (706) 695-2598, **Web: www.gastateparks.org**
- Hours: Tuesday-Saturday 9:00am-5:00pm, Sunday 2:00-5:30pm. Closed Monday (except holidays), Thanksgiving, Christmas and New Years. Closed Tuesday when open Monday.
- Admission: $2.00-$3.00 per person.

Known as the "Showplace of the Cherokee Nation," the brick mansion was built in 1804 by Chief James Vann, a Cherokee political leader and wealthy plantation owner. "Feared by many and loved by few," Vann was both a hero and a brute. On tour, you'll even see where he fired a pistol at dinner guests through the floor of the upstairs bedroom. The painted walls within the house represent colors of the earth, sky and harvest. Even President James Monroe stayed here. Their children played Cherokee stickball which is a smaller version of lacrosse. Chief Vann's greatest gift to the Cherokee Nation was the establishment of Springhouse Moravian Mission School. Although the missionaries were interested in bringing the gospel to the tribe, Vann saw an opportunity to educate Cherokee children. The Chief's son, Joseph, became an educated businessman and instrumental voice in the Cherokee legislature. However "Rich Joe" was forced off his property in 1835 at the beginning of the Cherokee removal process.

FORT MOUNTAIN STATE PARK

181 Fort Mountain Park Road (I-75 EXIT 333 toward GA 411 & GA 52)

Chatsworth 30705

- Phone: (706) 695-2621, **Web: www.gastateparks.org**
- Hours: Daily 7:00am-10:00pm.

Fort Mountain derives its name from an ancient 855-foot-long rock wall which stands on the highest point of the mountain. The mysterious wall is thought to have been built by Indians as a fortification against other more hostile Indians. Hikers and mountain bikers (14-30 miles) will find beautiful trails that wind through hardwood forest and blueberry thickets, occasionally crossing streams and vistas. For horseback riders, there are horse rentals, stables and 18 miles of trails. During the summer, families can enjoy the sand beach located on a cool mountain lake. 15 Cottages and several campsites are available as well as fishing and pedal boat rental or mini-golf.

PICKETT'S BATTLEFIELD STATE HISTORIC PARK

4432 Mt. Tabor Church Road (off GA 381, accessed by Dallas-Acworth Rd. or Due West Road)

Dallas 30157

- Phone: (770) 443-7850, **Web: www.gastateparks.org**
- Hours: Tuesday-Saturday 9:00am-5:00pm, Sunday Noon-5:00pm. Closed Monday (except holidays), Thanksgiving, Christmas and New Years.
- Admission: $1.25-$2.50
- Miscellaneous: Hiking trails and picnic sits. Battle Living History Encampment and Candle Lantern tours, annually.

Pickett's Mill is one of the best preserved Civil War battlefields in the nation. The scene of this bloody conflict looks much the same today as it did in 1864. Visitors may travel roads used by Federal and Confederate troops, see earthworks constructed by these men, and walk through the same ravine where hundreds died. The Confederate victory resulted in a one-week delay of the Federal advance on Atlanta. The Visitor Center is full of artifacts and exhibits relating to the battle and shows a film.

DALTON CARPET MILL TOURS

(I-75 exit 333 west one block)

Dalton 30722

- Phone: (706) 270-9960 or (800) 331-3258
  Web: www.daltoncvb.com
- Tours: Visitors can schedule a tour of a carpet mill by calling the CVB phone number.

A wedding gift started the carpet industry. When her brother married, young Catherine Evans Whitener wanted to get the happy couple a special gift...an heirloom bedspread. Catherine set about making one designed with a stitch that locked into the fabric when clipped and washed. Catherine called the stitch a "tuft". The bedspread was so liked by those who saw it that, later she began a cottage industry of making them to sell. The Singer Sewing Machine Company in nearby Chattanooga, Tennessee, took an interest and produced a machine to perform the task more efficiently. The product produced by machine were called "Chenille", the French word for "caterpillar", because the rows of machine-tufted threads resembled the creature. Pioneer businessmen experimented with the machines as a way to produce carpet. Their ideas worked. Today, Dalton is home to the multi-billion dollar carpet industry, making it the

"Carpet Capital of the World." See the giant carpet sewing machines that today produce modern carpet styles while on tour. If you want to see some of Catherine's original hand-tufted spreads, as well as chenille made by machine, visit the Hamilton House Museum in town.

CARLOS MUSEUM, MICHAEL C. AT EMORY UNIVERSITY

571 S. Kilgo Street

Decatur 30030

- Phone: (404) 727-4282, **Web: www.carlos.emory.edu**
- Hours: Tuesday-Saturday 10:00am-5:00pm, Sunday Noon-5:00pm, Thursdays until 9:00pm.
- Admission: $5.00 per person donation except Emory students and staff or museum members.
- Tours: Free docent-led tours of the Museum depart from the Rotunda on Level One every Thursday at 2:00pm and Sunday at 2:30pm.

The Carlos Museum offers a glimpse of 9,000 years of art history. From the wonders of ancient Greeks to modern architecture. The Art for All Ages and Art Activity for Children programs are best suited to families.

SOUTHWESTERN RAILWAY MUSEUM

3595 Peachtree Road (I-85 north of Atlanta, turn west past Gwinnett Place Mall and follow the signs)

Duluth 30096

- Phone: (770) 476-2013, **Web: www.srmduluth.org**
- Hours: Thursday, Friday, Saturday 10:00am-5:00pm (April-December). Saturdays only (January-March).
- Admission: $7.00 adult, $5.00 senior (65+), $4.00 child (2-12). Entry to exhibit hall and train rides included with admission.

Southwestern Railway Museum *(cont.)*

- Miscellaneous: this facility is not a glamorous site, but, instead a way to see restoration in progress.

See over 80 pieces of rolling stock, including vintage steam locomotives, historic wooden cars and Pullmans up close. Count how many beds are in the Sleeper/Lounge cars. Then, take as many short train rides aboard restored cabooses, as you like. We suggest standing out on the back platform.

CHICKAMAUGA BATTLEFIELD

(I-75 exit 350, then west on Hwy 2, south on 27, follow signs)

Fort Oglethorpe 30742

- Phone: (706) 866-9241
- Hours: Daily 8:30am-5:00pm. Park open until dusk. Closed Christmas.
- Admission: FREE

This is the site of the bloodiest two-day battle of the Civil War. In September, 1863, over 100,000 soldiers fought for control of Lafayette Road, resulting in 34,000 casualties. In the Visitor Center watch a multi-media presentation of the battle. The seven-mile tour route includes passing/stopping by: the Gordon-Lee Mansion (home headquarters to US General William Rosecrans - now open by appt. - it's a bed & breakfast); Lee and Gordon's Mill (station for General Braggs Confederate forces before the battle, stronghold station for General Rosecrans during the battle to prevent Confederates from crossing Chickamauga Creek).

ATLANTA MOTOR SPEEDWAY

1500 Tara Place (I-75 South to Exit #235 (15 miles South of downtown Atlanta) and continue on U.S. Highway 19 & 41 for 15 miles)

Hampton 30228

- Phone: (770) 707-7904 or (770) 707-7970 (tours)
  Web: www.gospeedway.com
- Tours: daily and run every half hour during operating hours (Monday-Saturday 9:00am-4:30pm, Sunday 1:00-4:30pm). Tours are just $5.00 adult and $2.00 child. Ages 6 and under are free.

Thrill to the excitement of NASCAR racing and special racing events watched around the world. Twice a year, Atlanta Motor Speedway is the bustling center of the NASCAR NEXTEL Cup world, filled with hundreds of thousands of fans from all over the country. But the rest of the year, this premier racing facility is open to the public for speedway tours and a behind-the-scenes look. TOURS: Official track tours include a brief track history, a visit to Petty Garden, a tour of one the track's luxury suites, a sneak peek at the garages and Victory Lane and two laps in the Speedway van around the same 1.54-mile track where stars like Jeff Gordon and Dale Earnhardt Jr. race. Track tours are available.

ROAD TO TARA MUSEUM

104 N. Main Street (housed in the 1867 Jonesboro Depot Welcome Center, by the tracks, downtown)

Jonesboro 30236

- Phone: (770) 478-4800
- Hours: Monday-Friday 8:30am-5:30pm, Saturday 10:00am-4:00pm.
- Admission: $5.00 adult, $4.00 senior and student.

Road To Tara Museum *(cont.)*

The museum is a must-see for Gone With The Wind fans from all over the world. Visitors to Jonesboro enjoy a look back at an era made famous by Margaret Mitchell's novel. Original props, costume reproductions, complete collectible plate and doll collections, a foreign edition library and an extensive photo gallery offer a glimpse into the writing of the book and making of the movie. Reading the book or watching the long movie is a must before visiting. We'd recommend tweeners on up.

KENNESAW MOUNTAIN NATIONAL BATTLEFIELD PARK

(I-75 exit 269, Barrett Pkwy, follow signs)

Kennesaw 30144

- Phone: (770) 427-4686
- Hours: Daily 8:30am-5:00pm.

This important battle brought General Sherman's march toward Atlanta to a halt for two weeks. Atop Kennesaw Mountain is an observation platform and memorial to 14 Confederate generals. Inside the Visitor Center, view interpretive showcases and a film. Outside, original earthworks and Civil War artillery can be viewed along marked trails.

SOUTHERN MUSEUM OF CIVIL WAR AND LOCOMOTIVE HISTORY

2829 Cherokee Street NW (I-75 exit 273 west)

Kennesaw 30144

- Phone: (770) 427-2117 or (800) 742-6897
  Web: www.southernmuseum.org

- Hours: Monday-Saturday 9:30am-5:00pm, Sunday Noon-5:00pm. Closed New Years, Easter, Thanksgiving and Christmas.
- Admission: $7.50 adult, $6.50 senior (60+), $5.50 child (6-12)

The true story behind the old Disney movie, "The Great Locomotive Chase," is what the Southern Museum is all about. The museum's star attraction is The General, a steam locomotive nabbed by Yankee raiders in 1862 just 100 yards from where it stands today. The daring band of 22 planned to drive The General north to Chattanooga and destroy Confederate supply lines along the way. Rebels manned a locomotive of their own and chased The General, full throttle, for 100 miles until the raiders were forced to abandon ship. Most were captured. Unfortunately for Kennesaw, a few thousand of their friends came back two years later. The Battle of Kennesaw Mountain that followed was one of the bloodiest conflicts fought during the 1864 Atlanta Campaign.

YELLOW RIVER GAME RANCH

4525 Highway 78 (I285 exit 39B), **Lilburn** 30047

- Phone: (770) 972-6643
  Web: www.yellowrivergameranch.com
- Hours: Daily 9:30am-6:00pm.
- Admission: $7.00 adult, $6.00 child (3-11).

Visit with more than 600 friendly animals that enjoy food and petting. There are deer, bear, mountain lion, bobcat, bear, farm animals, ducks and squirrels living along the naturally wooded path by the river. There's the "Billy Goat Gruff Memorial Bridge" and the super popular "Bunny Burrows." They even have one of the largest herd of buffalo east of the Mississippi, roaming in the back meadow. Don't forget to stop by and say "hello" to General Beauregard Lee, Georgia's official groundhog weather predictor!

SWEETWATER CREEK STATE CONSERVATION PARK

Mount Vernon Road (follow signs from I-20 exit 44, Thornton Road)

Lithia Springs 30057

- Phone: (770) 732-5871, **Web: www.gastateparks.org**
- Hours: Trails close at dark; other areas close at dark if not in use. Park opens at 7:00am, daily.
- Admission: $2.00 per vehicle.

Only minutes from bustling downtown Atlanta, nine miles of wooded trails follow the free-flowing stream to the ruins of the New Manchester Manufacturing Company, a textile mill burned during the Civil War. Beyond the mill, the trail climbs rocky bluffs to provide views of the beautiful shoals below. The 215-acre George Sparks Reservoir is popular for fishing, feeding ducks and canoeing. Fishing supplies & snacks are available in the park's bait shop, while maps & park information may be found in the Visitor Center.

NOAH'S ARK ANIMAL REHABILITATION CENTER

712 L G Griffin Road (I-75 exit 212), **Locus Grove** 30248

- Phone: (770) 937-0888, **Web: www.noahs-ark.org**
- Hours: Tuesday-Saturday Noon-3:00pm.
- Admission: FREE

This lovingly guided center primarily provides pet therapy as neglected and abused animals and children help to heal each other. The center houses rehabilitated and exotic animals such as lions, tigers, bears and monkeys. Some reptiles and raptors appear on occasion. The general public are invited to visit the nature trails and animal habitats at no charge. Be sure to view their informational video online or in person to understand the good work they are committed to. Maybe consider a family donation to help their cause?

REYNOLDS MEMORIAL NATURE PRESERVE

5665 Reynolds Road (I-75 exit 233, left onto Jonesboro Road. Go 1.5 miles to Huie Road and turn left)

Morrow 30260

- Phone: (770) 603-4188
  Web: http://web.co.clayton.ga.us/reynolds/about.htm
- Hours: The Nature Center is open Monday-Friday 8:30am-5:30pm, first Saturday of each month 9:00am-1:00pm.
- Admission: FREE

The preserve's primarily hardwood forest boasts ponds, wetlands, streams, designated picnic areas and four miles of well defined foot paths. The paths are laid out in convenient loops which bring visitors back to their starting point. The preserve's gardens include a heritage vegetable and herb garden featuring varieties from the late 1800's, a butterfly and hummingbird garden, and a native plants garden. The Georgia Native Plants Trail is wheelchair accessible. Inside the Nature Center you'll find a collection of native amphibians and reptiles as well as an observation honeybee hive and environmental education exhibits.

SUN VALLEY BEACH

5350 Holloman Road

Powder Springs 30127

- Phone: (770) 943-5900, **Web: www.sunvalleybeach.com**
- Hours: Daily 10:00am-8:00pm (summers, mid-May to mid-August). Weekends only 2 weeks before/after summer schedule.
- Admission: $16.00 adult, $10.00 senior, $14.00 child.

This family waterpark and spacious recreation destination is home to the Southeast's largest swimming facility, one and a half acres in size. The pool has 10 water slides, a dolphin fountain, showering umbrella, Lumber Jack log roll, diving platforms, and two rope swings. The "pool" is surrounded by a white sandy beach, volleyball courts, sports fields, and picnic areas.

CLOUDLAND CANYON STATE PARK

122 Cloudland Canyon Park Road (on GA 136, 8 miles east of Tenton and I-59)

Rising Fawn 30738

- Phone: (706) 657-4050, **Web: www.gastateparks.org**
- Hours: Daily 7:00am-10:00pm.
- Admission: FREE

Located on the western edge of Lookout Mountain, this scenic parks offers rugged geology and beautiful vistas. With elevation differing from 800 to 1,980 feet, the most spectacular views into the canyon are found near the picnic area parking lot. However, additional views can be found along the rim trail. Rugged hikers might want to walk to the bottom of the gorge to find two waterfalls cascading over layers of sandstone and shale. Cottages are located near the canyon edge, where the park's walk-in campsites provide privacy, too.

CHIEFTAINS MUSEUM

501 Riverside Parkway (between GA 53 & US 27)

Rome 30161

- Phone: (706) 291-9494, **Web: www.chieftainsmuseum.org**
- Hours: Tuesday-Friday 9:00am-3:00pm, Saturday 10:00am-4:00pm. Closed Sunday, Monday and all major holidays.
- Admission: $1.50-$3.00

The Museum tells the story of Major Ridge, the prominent Cherokee leader who struggles to adapt to the white man's culture while retaining his Cherokee heritage. Located on the banks of the Oostanaula River, Ridge and his family became ferryboat masters, store owners and slave-owning planters nearby. The white clapboard plantation home contains exhibits describing Ridge's life and the history of the Cherokee people.

STONE MOUNTAIN PARK

(I-285 exit 39B, US 78, follow signs)

Stone Mountain 30086

- Phone: (770) 498-5690 or (800) 317-2006
  Web: www.stonemountainpark.com
- Hours: Most open at 10:00am, closing between 5:00-8:00pm. Weather conditions may affect operating schedules.
- Admission: Entrance into Stone Mountain Park requires a $8.00 one day permit per vehicle. This permit gives you access to many of the Park's amenities including the public picnic areas, nature trails, children's playground, walk-up trail and the Lasershow Spectacular. All day passes suggested for most every activity: $16.00-$19.00 (age 3+). Duck Adventure: $9.00-$13.00 extra. Discounted during some winter days.
- Miscellaneous: Crossroads 1870s theme town, Gristmill picnic area, park lodges, pedal boats, Antique Car Museum, Paddleboat Cruises, covered bridge, hiking/nature trails, mini-golf, boat rentals, Beach & Waterslide complex, Interactive Play Barn, and several theme restaurants serving buffets and Southern-style sandwiches and chicken dishes. Note: A day or two is easily had at this wonderful attraction that meets or beats expectations.

Stone Mountain Park offers so much family fun (and adventure, too!). Here's just some of the lineup:

STONE MOUNTAIN: The world's largest exposed mass of granite has a Confederate Memorial carving that is larger than the size of a football field! When workers were carving, they would hide from the elements in the carved horses' mouths. Skylift: takes guests to the top. Once on top, walk out onto the top and sides of the mountain! It looks like giant moon craters up there! A must do! Exhilarating!

LASERSHOW SPECTACULAR: a modern laser animation projection system transforms brilliant, colorful lights into dramatic stories, historic tales and all sorts of comical characters. With a state-of-the-art surround sound system, dazzling fireworks and a flame cannon shooting fireballs hundreds of feet into the air…this is a great way to end your day. Bring a blanket, grab a snack and lounge chairs and gaze at the evening mountainside. (Nightly each summer, Saturdays only in Spring and Fall)

SCENIC RAILROAD: Open air cars with a wonderful, simple history narration.

RIDE THE DUCKS ADVENTURE. A 40 minute tour, on land and in water, throughout the Park. The tour includes interesting information about the Park, Atlanta and Georgia – presented by the Duck Captain in a fun and unforgettable way! The vehicle is commonly known as a "Duck," an amphibious vehicle (can move from land to water) used in the WWII era. Each guest aboard is provided with their very own Wacky Quacker™ for the ride.

TREEHOUSE CHALLENGE: This cool outdoor attraction has two dueling tree houses, where boys and girls join forces to compete against the opposite gender for bragging rights. Each tree house stretches three stories high and gives kids over three dozen interactive activities and challenges to enjoy.

<u>CONFEDERATE HALL HIST'L & ENVIRONMENTAL EDUCATION CENTER</u>: Educate local students and Park guests about the fascinating geology and ecology of Stone Mountain. "War in Georgia" large screen video format movie.

JAMES H. "SLOPPY" FLOYD STATE PARK

2800 Sloppy Floyd Lake Road (3 miles SE of town via US 27)

Summerville 30747

- Phone: (706) 857-0826, **Web: www.gastateparks.org**
- Hours: Daily 7:00am-10:00pm.
- Admission: FREE. Camping and cottage fees.

This quiet park in northwest Georgia offers outstanding fishing on two stocked lakes. Visitors can hike along three miles of lake loop trails and relax in swings while watching for the many bluebirds that live in the park. Children like the playground, feeding fish from the boardwalk and renting pedal boats. A small campground and a few cottages are nestled on tree-covered hillsides.

FUNK HERITAGE CENTER

7300 Reinhardt College Circle (on Reinhardt College campus)

Waleska 30183

- Phone: (770) 720-5970 or (770) 720-5971
  Web: www.reinhardt.edu/funk.htm
- Hours: Monday-Friday 9:00am-4:00pm, Saturday 10:00am-5:00pm, Sunday 1:00-5:00pm. Closed major holidays.
- Admission: $6.00 adult, $5.50 senior, $4.00 child.
- Tours: Guided tours of the museum take 90 minutes, by reservation, for groups.

Notice the contemporary building inspired by Indian designs. The museum interprets the story of the Southeastern

Indians and the early Appalachian settlers through interactive displays, dioramas and exhibits of contemporary Native American art. On the outside grounds is a recreated early 19th century settlers' village. Can you guess how each of the thousands of tools for craft and trade are used?

WEINMAN MINERAL MUSEUM

51 Mineral Museum Drive (I-75 North to Exit 293)

White 30184

- Phone: (770) 386-0576, **Web: www.weinmanmineral.org**
- Hours: Monday-Saturday 10:00am-5:00pm. Closed most national holidays.
- Admission: $3.00-$4.00 (age 6+).

Minerals or "rocks" are very important natural resources for Bartow County. William Weinman, for whom the museum is named, was a Barite miner. Barite is used in the manufacture of rubber for tennis balls, golf balls, brake shoes, eye glasses & much more. The largest exhibit contains a fossil dig filled with real and replicated bones, shark teeth, trilobites, and more. Specimens in the museum are likely to generate questions and comments. When kids look at Okenite (from India), you'll hear comments like "cotton balls" and "fuzzy". Okenite is soft, and touching it will destroy its delicate fibers. Try to find the "fuzzy rock" on your visit to the museum!

SUGGESTED LODGING AND DINING

DALTON DEPOT RESTAURANT & TRACKSIDE CAFÉ. 110 Depot Street (I-75 exit 333, go east on Walnut to left on Thorton. Right on Crawford, left on Hamilton and then one block to Kings St), (706) 226-3160. The Western & Atlantic Depot of the 1850s served as a Confederate army ordinance depot during the war. Surrounding the interior is a lengthy mini-railroad track with trains running. Kids can push button control the lobby display. Speaking of trains, you will likely hear a real one go by as you dine (maybe even 3-4 trains). Children's Menu $3.95, Dinners run $10.00-$16.00. Hours: Open for lunch and dinner, Tuesday-Saturday.

HAMPTON INN OF DALTON. 1000 Market Street (I-75 exit 333). (706) 226-4333. The hotel has a complimentary large hot/cold breakfast with new foods introduced each morning plus fresh fruits. There is also an outdoor pool and an indoor spa. It's located next to an outlet center, Cracker Barrel, Dairy Queen and many other restaurants and shopping within walking distance.

Chapter 5
South East Area - (SE)

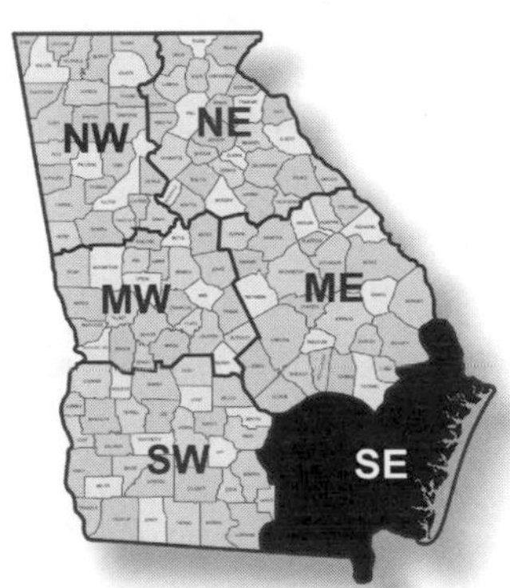

Our Favorites...

* Sapelo Island Geechee Tour - Darien (Sapelo Island)
* Dolphin Sightseeing Tours - Islands
* Bicycling - Jekyll Island
* Juliette Gordon Low Birthplace - Savannah
* Trolley Tours - Savannah, St. Simon's
* Tybee Island Marine Science Center & Beach Pier
* Okefenokee Swamp Park - Waycross

Cast Net Fishing - Sapelo Island

EARTH DAY NATURE TRAIL

One Conservation Way

Brunswick 31520

- Phone: (912) 264-7218
  Web: www.dnr.state.ga.us/dnr/coastal/
- Hours: Daily sunrise to sunset.
- Admission: FREE
- Miscellaneous: Groups, call ahead for access to video and outdoor classroom facilities for teaching.

The Earth Day Nature Trail was designed to be a self-guided educational activity. The trail features an osprey and eagle nesting platform, a wading-bird habitat, wildlife observation decks and observation tower.

MARY MILLER DOLL MUSEUM

209-211 Gloucester Street (downtown)

Brunswick 31520

- Phone: (912) 267-7569
- Hours: Monday-Friday 10:00am-4:30pm.

There are over 3,500 dolls, toys, and accessories representing over 90 countries and over 150 years of history on display at this doll museum that features pre-Civil War china heads, bisques, early vinyls, and carved wooden pieces. Mostly look, don't touch, behind glass cases, this is a dream to view for avid doll lovers. Admission required.

MARY ROSS WATERFRONT PARK

(Brunswick Harbor Market at the end of Gloucester Street)

Brunswick 31520

- Hours: Daylight
- Admission: FREE

A scaled-down replica of the WWII workhorse ship, the Liberty Ship is docked here. The park also has outdoor musical playscape (make music on the playground equipment), staged pavilion, farmers market and amphitheater. Brunswick is one of the shrimp capitals of the world. The shrimp fleet may be seen from Bay Street (US 341) between Gloucester and Prince Streets - best late afternoon when the ships come in.

HOFWYL-BROADFIELD PLANTATION STATE HISTORIC SITE

US Hwy 17 North (I-95 exit 42 east on US 17)

Brunswick 31525

- Phone: (912) 264-7333, **Web: www.gastateparks.org**
- Hours: Tuesday-Saturday 9:00am-5:00pm, Sunday 2:00-5:30pm. Last main house tour 45 minutes before closing. Closed Monday except holidays.
- Admission: $2.00-$5.00

Around 1807, what was once a vast cypress swamp gave way to a man named Brailsford who carved from the terrain a rice plantation along the banks of the Altamaha River. Some 350 slaves worked the highly productive venture until war, hurricanes and the abolition of slavery caused its decline. Visitors today can see a model of a busy rice plantation, furnishings, and a brief film on the plantation's history before walking a short trail to the antebellum home.

The site also includes a nature trail that leads back to the Visitor Center along the edge of the marsh where rice once flourished.

FORT KING GEORGE

P O Box 711 (I-95 exit 49 east)

Darien 31305

- Phone: (912) 437-4770, **Web: www.gastateparks.org**
- Hours: Tuesday-Saturday 9:00am-5:00pm, Sunday 2:00-5:30pm. Closed Mondays (except holidays) and winter holidays.

From 1721 until 1736, Fort King George was the southern outpost of the British Empire in North America. His Majesty's Independent Company garrisoned the fort. They endured incredible hardships from disease, threats from the Spanish and Indian nations, and the harsh, unfamiliar coastal environment. After the fort was abandoned, General James Oglethorpe brought Scottish Highlanders to the site in 1736. The settlement eventually became the town of Darien and saw milling became a major industry. Walk around a fort replica as well as remains of three sawmills and tabby ruins.

SAPELO ISLAND - GEECHEE COMMUNITY TOUR

Sapelo Island Visitors Center (35 minutes north of Brunswick, US 17 to Darien, go east on GA 99 to Meridian, follow signs to ferry and Reserve), **Darien (Sapelo Island)** 31305

- Phone: (912) 437-3224
  Web: http://gastateparks.org/info/sapelo/
- Hours: Center: Tuesday-Friday 7:30am-5:30pm, Saturday 8:00am-5:30pm, Sunday 1:30-5:00pm.
- Admission: 1/2 day tours: $10.00 adult, $6.00 child (6-12).

Sapelo Island - Geechee Community Tour *(cont.)*

- Tours: Half- and full-day tours Wednesday 8:30am-12:30pm (mansion and Island) and Saturday 9:00am-1:00pm (lighthouse and island). An additional tour is offered Friday 8:30am-12:30pm (lighthouse and island) - summer only. Extended tour offered the last Tuesday of the Month (March-October), 8:30am-3:00pm (lighthouse, mansion and island). Reservations are required.
- Miscellaneous: Check in at the Visitors Center where you can orient to the area via displays on the history and culture of this remote island. Pack a backpack with snacks and water or purchase food at the small café on the island (a stop on the tour). Bicycles aren't allowed on DNR ferry rides, but you may rent bikes on the island. Campgrounds and group lodging.

This unique, undeveloped barrier island is one of the last places where the Geechee culture is lovingly maintained by residents, many of whom are the descendants of slaves. The similarities that link the cultures of Georgia's sea islands and the Windward Rice Coast of West Africa are generally referred to as the "Gullah Connection." Geechee distinguishes the language and slaves of Coastal Georgia. Gullah dialects, which combine English with the languages of African tribes, is still somewhat spoken here. During the guided tour of the island you will visit the antebellum mansion or the restored lighthouse, depending on the day that you visit. You'll see virtually every facet of a barrier island's natural community, from the forested uplands, to the vast salt marsh, and the complex beach and dunes systems. We learned and saw: ruins of a sugar mill; sampling leaves from a Toothache Tree (Prickly Ash) - we bit them and then rubbed it on our tongue or gums - it numbs it!; talked with natives, especially chatting with Geechee woman, Cornelia for a story or two; casting a net and examining your catch; stop at the Post Office and mail yourself a postcard from the Island; exploring the Reynolds Mansion (highlights were the solarium, gameroom and circus ballroom - want to spend a couple of nights? You can – group rates are available!); climbing the winding stairs of the lighthouse; and finally, exploring the beach or wading in the water. Like sand dollars and starfish? You can collect gobs of them as a souvenirs!

STEPHEN C. FOSTER STATE PARK

Route 1, Box 131 (18 miles northeast of town via GA 177)

Fargo 31631

- Phone: (912) 637-5274, **Web: www.gastateparks.org**
- Hours: Daily 7:00am- dark.
- Admission: FREE. Fee for camping , cottages and boat tours ($6.00-$8.00, call for times).

Named after songwriter Stephen Foster, this remote park is a primary entrance to the famed Okefenokee Swamp. Moss-laced cypress trees reflect off the black swamp waters and visitors can look for alligators, turtles, raccoon, black bear, deer and hundreds of species of birds while on the park's elevated boardwalk. Take the guided boat trip or (for the more adventurous), rent motorized boats or canoes for further exploration of the swamp, including a trip to historic Billy's Island. The park contains an Interpretive Center and Museum, cottages and modern campgrounds.

FOLKSTON FUNNEL TRAIN WATCHING PLATFORM

103 N. First Street

Folkston 31537

- Phone: (912) 496-2536
- Hours: More than 60 trains pass through this spot each day.

The "Folkston Funnel" is a double track which serves as the main artery for railroad traffic into and out of Florida. From the viewing platform in Folkston, visitors can see trains passing on their way to and from Florida in the south, and a split north of town where trains go west and north. The trains traveling through Folkston carry automobiles, coal, gravel, phosphate, grain, molten sulphur, and orange juice. Several Amtrak trains pass daily, including the Autotrain. The lighted platform features a scanner to listen in to radio traffic between trains. Adjacent to the platform are picnic tables, a grill, and a new restroom facility. Trains can also be enjoyed from the grounds of the restored Folkston depot, just diagonally across the tracks from the platform. Most folks who have visited this site claim it's one of the best viewing areas anywhere.

OKEFENOKEE NATIONAL WILDLIFE REFUGE

Okefenokee Parkway (8 miles southwest of town on SR 121/23, then 4 miles west of main entrance)

Folkston 31537

- Phone: (912) 496-7836, **Web: http://okefenokee.fws.gov**
- Hours: Daily sunrise to sunset.
- Admission: General Admission Fee is $5.00 per vehicle.

This swamp remains one of the oldest and most well preserved freshwater areas in America. Okefenokee is a vast bog inside a huge, saucer-shaped depression that was once part of the ocean floor. Okefenokee is the derivative of the Indian words meaning "Land of the Trembling Earth". Peat deposits, up to 15 feet thick, cover much of the swamp floor. These deposits are so unstable in spots that one can cause trees and surrounding bushes to tremble by stomping the surface! Why are some swamp waters tea-colored?

ISLAND HISTORY CENTER

Stable Road (west end of island directly across from entrance to Island Club), **Jekyll Island** 31527

- Phone: (912) 635-4092

Take a brief walk through the American Indian history, past the Millionaire's era up to the present at the island. Simulate the first intercontinental phone call made using two old-fashioned pay phones. Or, light up the Archeological Mystery boxes and see what glows.

JEKYLL ISLAND BIKING

Beachview Drive (begins at mini golf)

Jekyll Island 31527

- Phone: (912) 635-2648 or (877) 4Jekyll
- Hours: Daily 9:00am to 5:00 to 7:00pm.
- Admission: Rentals: $3.00-$4.00 per hour or $10.00+ per day per bike. Helmets and child seats or baskets available. Georgia law requires children 13 and under to wear bike helmets. FREE if you bring your own bikes.
- Miscellaneous: Mini-golf $5.00 per game. Two courses.

More than 20 miles of paved paths circle the island, providing a scenic ride for both the serious cyclist and pleasure biker. Starting from the rentals by mini-golf, travel two miles along the beach with ocean views and dunes. Continue on the North Loop past canopies of live oaks. To extend the ride, take the path to your right by the gate past Villas by the Sea to meander through the Clam Creek area. You'll be right in the middle of a marsh. Loop around the fishing piers, down more canopies of oaks draped in Spanish Moss towards the Historic District. Once in the Historic District, continue straight toward Jekyll Island Club on road ahead. Pass behind the hotel, by Faith Chapel and Villa Marianna. Continue down Old Plantation Road and stop at the Island History Center. Want more forest environs? Head to South Loop near Tidelands Nature Center. Once through the forest, head out towards the Beach again and see "Glory" Beach, where the movie was filmed.

SUMMER WAVES WATER PARK

(next to the marsh on Riverview Drive)

Jekyll Island 31527

- Phone: (912) 635-2074, **Web: www.summerwaves.com**
- Hours: Vary by season. Daily from Memorial Day to Labor Day and on select weekends in May and September. Monday-Thursday 10:00am-6:00pm, Friday-Saturday 10:00am-8:00pm, Sunday 11:00am-7:00pm.
- Admission: $15.00-$17.00 (age 4+). $10.00 senior (60+).
- Miscellaneous: Changing areas, restrooms and eateries are available.

More than one million gallons of splashing water fun and 11 acres of rides. Gather your courage for the Pirates Passage, a totally enclosed speed flume that jets riders over three humps in total darkness or the Force 3 inner tube flume. Or, catch a wave in the Frantic Atlantic wave pool and enjoy a lazy inner tube ride on Turtle Creek. For kids under 48" tall, Summer Waves kiddie pool offers carefully supervised water playgrounds complete with slides and waterfalls in just 12 inches of bubbling water. (inner tubes and life vests are provided throughout the park at no charge).

TIDELANDS NATURE CENTER

100 Riverview Drive (next to Summer Waves Water Park)

Jekyll Island 31527

- Phone: (912) 635-5032, **Web: www.tidelands4h.org**
- Hours: Monday-Saturday 9:00am-4:00pm, Sunday 10:00am-2:00pm
- Admission: Suggested $1.00 donation.

Have you ever touched a live seashell? Now you can. Stop by and visit a young sea turtle, corn snake, fish, alligators and other species native to Georgia's coast. Aquariums and touch tanks on site specialize in the local ecosystems. Touch a starfish and many crabs - even pet turtles. The touch box room is a stop for kids (near the end so they can apply what they've learned). Our favorite part has to be the hatchling loggerhead turtles that are being raised here. You'll be mesmerized as they watch you and show off their giraffe-like legs, thick "log" neck and pretty yellow, orange and brown color. (Note: if you can't go out looking for turtle nests - they have a great diorama of a mother nesting that shows the instinctive habit they have every summer). There is also a self-guide nature trail. Sign up for nature walks to the beach or marsh. Maybe even go seining - kick off your shoes and learn to use a seine net to capture creatures in the surf.

TURTLE WALKS, THE SEA TURTLE PROJECT

100 Stable Road (Island History Center departures)

Jekyll Island 31527

- Phone: (912) 635-2284 or 912-635-4036 Center
  Web: www.jekyllisland.com/what/turtles.html
- Admission: Depends on tour.

Turtle Walks, The Sea Turtle Project *(cont.)*

- Tours: 8:30 and 9:30pm (June thru mid-August). Any age is welcome with a parent; children over age 12 can participate unattended with parental permission.
- Miscellaneous: Video presentation and exhibits detail the history of the island from the native inhabitants to the present.

Under a cover of darkness, female Loggerhead sea turtles swim ashore, make their way across the sand, dig their nests and lay their eggs. Designated a threatened species by state and federal law, loggerhead sea turtles have found safe haven on Jekyll Island. Their nests, tucked among the dunes of Island beaches are the treasure find of the tours. Following a description of sea turtles and their habitat, local wildlife guides conduct shoreline walks in search of turtle tracks and nesting mothers. From a safe distance, participants view the fascinating pageant of life as 80-100 eggs are deposited in the nest.

GENERAL COFFEE STATE PARK

46 John Coffee road (6 miles east of Douglas on GA 32)

Nicholls 31554

- Phone: (912) 384-7082, **Web: www.gastateparks.org**
- Hours: Daily 7:00am-10:00pm.
- Admission: FREE. Fee for camping and cottages.

This park is known for interpretation of agricultural history at its Heritage Farm, with log cabins, a corn crib, cane mill, barnyard animals, tobacco barn and others. A 17-mile river winds through a cypress swamp where the park harbors rare and endangered plants. The threatened indigo snake and gopher tortoise make their homes in this longleaf pine/wiregrass natural area. Overnight accommodations include camping and cottages. Their 4 mile hiking trails include nature trails and a boardwalk. The river dock rents canoe and pedal boats.

MIGHTY EIGHTH AIR FORCE HERITAGE MUSEUM

147 Bourne Avenue (I-95 exit 102)

Pooler 31322

- Phone: (912) 748-8888, **Web: www.mightyeighth.org**
- Hours: Daily 9:00am-5:00pm.
- Admission: $10.00 adult, $9.00 senior, $6.00 child (6-12).

The museum honors the courage, character and patriotism embodied by the men and women of the Eighth Air Force from WWII to the present. You will be moved by the inspiring stories of heroism, courage, and sacrifice as well as remind us of the price that was paid for our freedom. Fly a bombing mission with a B-17 crew or view historic aircraft.

OGLETHORPE SPEEDWAY PARK

200 Jesup Road (I-95, use exit 102 (US Highway 80) and go east three miles)

Pooler 31322

- Phone: (912) 964-RACE, **Web: www.ospracing.net**

This NASCAR sanctioned park entertains thousands every weekend with stock car and go-cart racing. RV campground on site. View website for schedule and fees for each event.

FORT MCALLISTER STATE HISTORIC PARK

3894 Fort McAllister Road (10 miles east of I-95 on GA Spur 144, exit 90)

Richmond Hill 31324

- Phone: (912) 727-2339, **Web: www.gastateparks.org**
- Hours: 8:00am-5:00pm.
- Admission: $1.50-$2.50 per person.

The sand and mud earthworks were attacked seven times by Union ironclads, but did not fall until captured in 1864 by General Sherman during his infamous "March to the Sea". The museum interprets the best-preserved earthwork fortification of the Civil War using numerous themed displays. The interior design of the museum resembles a bombproof shelter and also contains a gift shop and shows a video on the history of the site regularly. This park is a quiet location for camping, hiking, fishing and picnicking. There are 4.3 miles of hiking and biking trails.

JULIETTE GORDON LOW BIRTHPLACE

10 East Oglethorpe Avenue (corner of Bull Street and Oglethorpe Avenue),

Savannah 31401

- Phone: (912) 233-4501, **Web: www.girlscouts.org/birthplace**
- Hours: Monday-Saturday 10:00am-4:00pm, Sunday 11:00-4:00pm. Closed Wednesday (September-February), major holidays and the first two weeks in January.
- Admission: $8.00 adult, $5.00 student (6-18), $20.00 family. Girl Scout adult chaperone $6.00, Girl Scout $4.00.
- Miscellaneous: Ask for the special visit Girl Scout pin at the Museum shop (about $3.50 to purchase). Guided tours begin every so often.

Juliette Gordon Low, founder of the Girl Scouts, is one of the most famous women in American history. She was born in Savannah, and her home serves as a Historic Landmark. Begin on a guided tour and hear firsthand about the Gordons, a great American family. From William Washington Gordon I, founder of the Central of Georgia Railroad, to his world famous granddaughter. Enjoy funny stories of the spirited "Nelly" Gordon (loved to slide down the curved staircase) and "Daisy" Low (Juliette, a creative artist - look for her sculpture and paintings throughout the house), multi-talented and quirky but severely hearing impaired, founded the organization of productive fun for young ladies. Why is the Boy Scout founder very connected to the founding of Girl Guides? "Come right over! I've got something for the girls of Savannah and all America and all the world and we're going to start it tonight!" - Juliette's famous words that started the Girl Scouts in 1912 to become one of the most significant organizations of the time. She gave the girls of America the career opportunities, outdoor activities and the fun they so desperately wanted.

MASSIE HERITAGE INTERPRETATION CENTER

207 East Gordon Street (Calhoun Square)

Savannah 31401

- Phone: (912) 201-5070, **Web: www.massieschool.com**
- Hours: Monday-Friday 9:00am-4:00pm. Simply ring the bell to the right of the front doors.
- Admission: $3.00 self-guided tour. $5.00 guided tour. Ages 4+.

Massie Heritage Interpretation Center *(cont.)*

The old school house provides group participation including the:

- HERITAGE CLASSROOM - You can experience lessons just like those of students a hundred or more years ago… sit up straight and place your folded hands on top of your desk. Lessons include oral recitation and even penmanship using real quill pens. Do your arithmetic and take your spelling test using a slate board.
- SAVANNAH'S CITY PLAN - It is the old city of Savannah as it developed according to James Edward Oglethorpe's plan from 1733 to 1856 when all of the publicly owned land was used up.
- THE DEBATABLE LANDS - Over a span of 12,000 years, Native Americans built villages and forts, burial grounds and playgrounds, and summer and winter camps. When Europeans finally arrived, they built their towns on or near these earlier inhabited sites. The space informs visitors about the history of Chatham County and Coastal Georgia prior to Oglethorpe's arrival in 1733.

Also, displays on the Victorian Era and Classical architecture are covered.

ROUNDHOUSE RAILROAD MUSEUM

601 W. Harrris Street (adjacent to the Savannah Info ctr, downtown)

Savannah 31401

- Phone: (912) 651-6823
  Web: www.chsgeorgia.org/roundhouse/
- Hours: Daily 9:00am-5:00pm.
- Admission: $4.00 adult, $3.50 senior, student, Free (6 under)

Originally designed to transport valuable Georgia cotton, the 190 miles of rail line between Savannah and Macon completed by 1843 formed the longest continuous railroad under one management in the world. The site remains a tribute to the 19th century Industrial Revolution. The site includes a massive roundhouse with operating turntable, a 125 foot restored smokestack, the oldest portable steam engine in the US, and an HO scale model of Savannah.

SAVANNAH HISTORY MUSEUM

303 Martin Luther King Jr. (adjacent to the Savannah Info Center)

Savannah 31401

- Phone: (912) 238-1779, **Web: www.chsgeorgia.org/shm/**
- Hours: Daily 9:00am-5:00pm
- Admission: $4.00 adult, $3.50 senior, military, student, $3.00 child (6-11).
- Miscellaneous: Old Savannah Tours - (912) 234-8128 or (800) 517-9007 or **www.oldsavtour.com**. Voted Savannah's best tour in 2003, this locally owned and operated company offers all-day, unlimited on/off, and sightseeing tours. Open-air trolleys escort you around the town's history.

This museum is housed in the old railroad passenger train shed. Museum exhibits include an 1800 cotton gin, Central of Georgia steam locomotive Baldwin #403, Juliette Gordon Low's family carriage and Forrest Gump's bench (with picks from the movie and even his little suitcase). An 18-minute video overview of Savannah explains the founding of the city from founding father, Oglethorpe's point of view (excellent start to tour) and a diorama depicts the siege of attacks on the city.

SAVANNAH TROLLEY TOURS, GRAY LINE

(we suggest starting from the Visitors Ctr located on MLK Blvd)

Savannah 31401

- Phone: (912) 284-Tour or (800) 426-2318
  Web: www.graylineofsavannah.com
- Admission: $19.00 adult, $8.00 child (5-11).
- Tours: Daily 9:00am-4:30pm (leave every 20 minutes)

The official daily tours of the Historic Foundation have more than 20 departures daily through the Historic district and Low Country. You'll see and hear about: The film "Glory" production site in old Revolutionary War ruins; The Mary Ghost of Telfair - she doesn't permit food or beverage in the Telfair Art Museum; "Forrest Gump" famous bench site (the bench can be seen in the History center); Sherman's Headquarters where he promised not to burn Savannah; A 400 year old live oak tree; A Real Pirate's House Inn (you might want to avoid this place if you lived in the 1800s - you might have ended up on a pirate boat as a slave); and, pass the founder of the Girl Scouts birthplace. This is absolutely the best way to survey Savannah's numerous historic sites and squares and shops. Start your stay in the city on tour.

OLD FORT JACKSON NATIONAL HISTORIC PARK

1 Fort Jackson Road (2 miles east of downtown)

Savannah 31404

- Phone: (912) 232-3945, **Web: www.chsgeorgia.org/shm/**
- Hours: Daily 9:00am-5:00pm
- Admission: $4.00 adult, $3.00 senior (55+), military, student.

This fort is the oldest remaining brickwork fort. The fort first saw service in the War of 1812 and then again during the Civil War. This fort guards Five Fathom Hole, the 18th century deep-water port in the Savannah River. The fort displays artifacts depicting the history of town and Coastal Georgia. Seasonal demonstrations and exhibits are scheduled for the second weekend of each month.

WORMSLOE STATE HISTORIC SITE

7601 Skidaway Road (10 miles southeast of Savannah's historic district), **Savannah** 31406

- Phone: (912) 353-3023, **Web: www.wormsloe.org**
- Hours: Tuesday-Saturday 9:00am-5:00pm, Sunday 2:00-5:30pm. Closed Mondays except holidays.
- Admission: $1.50-$2.50 per person.

An avenue lined with live oaks leads to the tabby ruins of Wormsloe, the colonial estate constructed by Noble Jones, one of Georgia's first settlers. Jones was an English physician and carpenter who carved out an even wider career in the colonial wilderness. He came to Savannah with James Oglethorpe in 1733 and commanded a company of Marines, served as constable, Indian agent, surveyor and a member of the Royal Council. He was also one of the few original settlers to survive hunger, Indians and Spaniards in this new wilderness. Today, visitors can view artifacts excavated at the site and watch a film about the founding of the 13th colony. A scenic nature trail leads to the living history area where, during special programs, costumed staff show skills and crafts necessary to early settlers. The living history programs are the best time to visit as a family.

LOW COUNTRY RIVER EXCURSIONS

8005 Old Tybee Road (Bull River Marina, Hwy 80)

Savannah 31410

- Phone: (912) 898-9222, **Web: www.lowcountrycruise.com**
- Admission: $15.00 adult, $12.00 senior, $10.00 child (under 12)
- Tours: Noon, 2:00pm and 6:00pm (June-mid September). Departures 2:00pm and 4:00pm (April, May). 2:00pm (March & mid-September thru November). Reservations Recommended. Rest room and beverages on board.

Join an encounter with friendly Bottle Nose Dolphins. Enjoy the scenery and wildlife during the 90 minute cruise down Bull River aboard large pontoon boats.

OATLAND ISLAND EDUCATION CENTER

711 Sandtown Road (5 miles east of Savannah off Islands Expressway), **Savannah** 31410

- Phone: (912) 898-3980, **Web: www.oatlandisland.org**
- Hours: Monday-Friday 9:00am-4:00pm, Saturday 10:00am-4:00pm
- Admission: $3.00 per person (age 4+).

Located on a marsh island, the Center features a 2 mile "Native Animal Nature Trail" that winds through maritime forest, salt marsh, and freshwater wetlands. Along the way, visitors can observe native animals such as Florida panthers, Eastern timber wolves, alligators, bison and bears in their natural habitat. It is not unusual to see blue tailed (five-lined) skinks, neotropical birds, herons, hawks, raccoon tracks, or otter scat.

SKIDAWAY ISLAND STATE PARK

52 Diamond Causeway (I-16 to exit I-516 (#164A). Turn right on Waters Avenue and go straight ahead to Diamond Causeway)

Savannah 31411

- Phone: (912) 598-2300, **Web: www.gastateparks.org**
- Hours: Daily 7:00am-10:00pm.
- Admission: FREE. Camping fee.

With Savannah at one end and Tybee Island beaches nearby, this barrier island has both salt and fresh water due to estuaries and marshes that flow through the area. The park borders Skidaway Narrows, a part of the intracoastal waterway, and provides scenic camping and picnicking. Two nature trails wind through marshes, live oaks, cabbage-palmettos and longleaf pines. Watch for deer, raccoon and migrating birds. Observation towers provide another chance to search for wildlife. The interpretive center has a bird-viewing station and a giant Ground Sloth fossil replica.

UGA MARINE EDUCATION CENTER AND AQUARIUM

30 Ocean Science Circle (I-516 to town as it becomes DeRenne Ave. Right on Waters, changing to Whitfield, then Diamond Cseway. Go past State Pk, left on McWhorter 4 miles)

Savannah 31411

- Phone: (912) 598-FISH, **Web: www.uga.edu/aquarium**
- Hours: Monday-Friday 9:00am-4:00pm, Saturday Noon-5:00pm.
- Admission: $1.00-$2.00 (age 3+).

The University of Georgia's public saltwater aquarium exhibits display organisms typical of the various habitats that are found along the coast: the tidal creeks of the salt marshes, the ocean beaches, and the open waters of the continental shelf including "live bottom" areas such as Gray's Reef National Marine Sanctuary. Fourteen exhibit tanks hold 200 live animals that represent approximately 50 species of fish, turtles, and invertebrates found along the Georgia coast. Look for sharks, whales, mastodons and mammoths dredged from the Skidaway River. Native American artifacts dating back to the "Guale" era of Georgia's prehistory are also on exhibit, as are sea island grass baskets crafted by the Gullah residents of Sapelo Island.

RIVER STREET RIVERBOAT COMPANY

(departing from Savannah's Historic River Street directly behind City Hall)

Savannah 31412

- Phone: (912) 232-6404 or (800) 786-6404
  Web: www.savannahriverboat.com
- Admission: Sightseeing Tours: $16.00 adult, $9.50 child (under 12). Luncheon: $28.00-$31.00 adult, $16.50-$2000 child. Dinner cruises more.
- Tours: One Hour Sightseeing: Daily once or twice an afternoon (March-November). Noon Luncheon cruises: Weekends at Noon (1 1/2 hrs.)

Relive a bygone era on board one of the replica paddle wheelers for a view of the sites from the water. Hear the Captain's intriguing tales and historic facts as you travel a river once used by industrialists and war maneuvers. Sit back and enjoy the view.

BAMBOO FARM AND COASTAL GARDEN

2 Canebrake Road (I-95 exit 94. Go east on GA 204 to Hwy 17 south exit. Travel for one mile)

Savannah 31419

- Phone: (912) 921-5460
  http://pubs.caes.uga.edu/caespubs/horticulture/coastalgarden/coastalgarden.htm
- Hours: Monday-Friday 9:00am-4:00pm. Closed weekends and major holidays.
- Admission: FREE (donations accepted).

The Bamboo Farm serves as a research and education center and houses a number of plant collections, gardens and research plots maintained by UGA staff. The Bamboo Farm is perhaps best known for its collection of more than 140 varieties of shade- and sun-loving bamboos. The oldest grove of bamboo on the property, the Giant Japanese Bamboo, was planted more than 100 years ago. The farm is the largest collection of bamboo available for public viewing in the U.S. Two display gardens, the Cottage Garden and the Xeriscape Garden, are housed at the Bamboo Farm. The Cottage Garden serves as a trial garden where old and new varieties of perennials, annuals and bulbs can be evaluated for their adaptability to the southeastern coastal climate and soil. The Xeriscape Garden demonstrates the seven principles of water-wise landscaping and is used to teach water conservation practices to local gardeners and landscapers.

SAVANNAH OGEECHEE CANAL MUSEUM AND NATURE CENTER

681 Fort Argyle Road (located off GA 204, only 2.3 miles west of I-95 at exit 94), **Savannah** 31419

- Phone: (912) 748-8068, **Web: www.socanalmuseum.com**
- Hours: Daily 9:00am-5:00pm.
- Admission: $1.00-$2.00 per person.

Discover the history of the Savannah Ogeechee Canal at this Museum. Visitors are able to view the remnants of Canal Locks 5 and 6 and see a replica gate and lock model. The Nature Center consists of 184 acres of river swamp, pine flatwoods, and sandhill habitat with low-impact walking trails (something we look for when hiking miles at a time) throughout the area. The Nature Center supports a diverse group of stationary and migratory birds as well as reptiles and other animal life. Kids especially love the gopher tortoise habitat. Studying State History? The Museum and Nature Center is home to Georgia's state tree, the live oak; Georgia's state flower, the Cherokee rose; Georgia's state wildflower, the wild azalea; and Georgia's state reptile, the gopher tortoise. The state bird, the brown thrasher, can also be seen around the Nature Center.

CROOKED RIVER STATE PARK

6222 Charlie Smith St. Highway (7 miles north of St. Mary's on GA 40 or 8 miles east of I-95 exit 3)

St. Marys 31558

- Phone: (912) 882-5256, **Web: www.gastateparks.org**
- Hours: Daily 7:00am-10:00pm.
- Admission: FREE

This park offers cozy facilities with views of salt marshes and Spanish moss-draped oaks. Campsites are surrounded by oaks, while cottages overlook the river. Hikers can explore the nature trails (4 miles), which winds through maritime forest and salt marsh. Visitors may venture to the nearby ruins of the tabby "McIntosh Sugar Works" mill, built around 1825 and later used as a starch factory during the Civil War. Just down the road is the ferry to famous Cumberland Island National Seashore known for secluded beaches. The park also has an Olympic-size pool and bathhouse and a miniature golf course.

CUMBERLAND ISLAND NATIONAL SEASHORE

(Ice House Museum is located at the Dungeness Dock on the Island. The inland museum is just blocks from the water)

St. Marys 31558

- Phone: (912) 882-4335 or (888) 817-3421
  Web: www.nps.gov/cuis/pphtml/facilities.html
- Hours: Ice House Museum: 8:00am-4:00pm daily. Mainland Museum: 1:00-4:00pm. Generally, two ferry departures per day operating.
- Admission: Day Use Fee: $4.00 per person/visit. Ferry Price (round trip): $15.00 adult, $12.00 senior (65+), and $10.00 child (12 and under).
- Miscellaneous: The ferry does not transport pets, bicycles, kayaks, or cars. Boating, camping, fishing and hiking are activities available on the island.

Cumberland Island is 17.5 miles long and totals 36,415 acres of which 16,850 are marsh, mud flats, and tidal creeks. It is well known for its sea turtles, wild turkeys, wild horses, armadillos, abundant shore birds, dune fields, maritime forests, salt marshes, and historic structures. Special Programs conducted by rangers (on the island) are at 4:00pm dockside each afternoon when the ferry is operating. The Mainland Museum is located on Osborne Street, two blocks from the waterfront. The museum houses a collection of artifacts from Cumberland Island to highlight the people of the island. The lives of Native Americans, African Americans, the Carnegie family as well as others who lived on the island in the 19th and 20th centuries are seen in the island environment. This is the first major effort to bring the island story to mainland facilities. Another portion of the total collection is still on display on the island.

ST. MARYS FAMILY AQUATIC CENTER

301 Herb Bauer Drive

St. Marys 31558

- Phone: (912) 673-8118
- Hours: Monday-Friday 11:00am-6:00pm, Saturday 10:00am-6:00pm, Sunday 1:00-6:00pm (May-August).
- Admission: Call for seasonal pricing.

This brand new 7 acre water play area has something for the whole family. Adults can relax in a tube as you float around the park in the endless river or get in some exercise swimming in the lap pool. There is also a two story tall slide full of twists and turns that is sure to be exciting. Kids over four feet tall can ride the big slide, but the big attraction for the little ones is the play pool with dozens of ways to squirt, spray and splatter your friends with gallons of water.

ST. MARY'S HISTORIC TRAM OR RAILWAY TOUR

406 Osborne Road

St. Marys 31558

- Phone: (800) 868-8687 OR (866) 386-8729

Toonerville Trolley - "See You In The Funny Papers!" This saying originated by Roy Crane in his 1935 "Wash Tubbs &

Easy" comic strip. The strip featured the many local personalities who used this railcar to commute from St. Marys to Kingsland in the late 1920s. Take a Historic ride through St. Mary's including historic 1800s churches. Call for Tram tours price and reservations. Or, ride on the Historic St. Mary's Railroad. The 1947 locomotive leaves Daily at 9:00am, 12:30pm and 3:00pm except for Christmas and Easter.

DOLPHIN TOURS - ST. SIMONS TRANSIT COMPANY

St. Simons Marina, **St. Simons Island** 31522

- Phone: (912) 635-3152
  Web: www.saintsimonstransit.com/dolphin_tours.htm
- Admission: $20.00 adult, $10.00 child (10 and under)
- Tours: 75 minutes long. Departures Tuesday-Saturday at 1:00pm, 3:00pm and 5:00pm. Sunday at 1:00pm. Leave from St. Simons Marina. See website for additional tours leaving from Jekyll Island Historic site marina/wharf.

See dolphin frolicking in their natural habitat as you explore the marshes, the sound and tidal rivers. Comfortable, shaded tour boats offer plenty of move-about room to get a great view of the dolphins. Cruise the inland waters, so it is never rough. You will also enjoy marvelous views of shrimp boats, local birds and wildlife. Adequate and comfortable seating allows a maximum of 40 passengers. The captain and crew share a relaxed overview of the coastal environment.

FORT FREDERICA / BLOODY MARSH BATTLE SITE

Rte. 9, Box 286C (off Sea Island Road, Battle site is 5 miles south of Fort), **St. Simons Island** 31522

- Phone: (912) 638-3639, **Web: www.nps.gove/fofr**
- Hours: Gates open at 8:00am. Museum: Daily 9:00am-5:00pm. Closed Christmas Day.
- Admission: $5.00/vehicle, $3.00/person on foot, bike, or bus.

When General James Oglethorpe claimed Georgia territory for England, it was important to build settlements within forts. He found this site on the river bank and named it Frederica. By the 1740s, Frederica was a thriving village of about 500 citizens. When Spanish troops sought to capture St. Simons Island in 1742, Oglethorpe's men won a decisive victory in what is now called The Battle of Bloody Marsh. In July of 1742, an outnumbered force of British troops ambushed and defeated Spanish troops, halting an attack aimed at Fort Frederica. The battle proved to be the turning point in the Spanish invasion of Georgia. By the late 1740s the fort was not needed and disbanded. Today, you can visit the site of Fort Frederica and see the ruins of the fortifications, barracks and homes. A museum, film, dioramas, tours, and demonstrations bring the settlement vividly to life.

GOLDEN ISLE KAYAK AND CANOE TRIPS

St. Simons Island 31522

Kayaks and canoes are great ways to explore the creeks and marshes of the Golden Isles. Many local outfitters offer instruction and can tailor customer outings to fit family needs and interests. Offered spring through fall.

- Ocean Motion, St. Simons Island, 912-638-5225.
- Barry's Beach Service, St. Simons Island, 912-638-8053.
- Southeast Adventure Outfitters, St. Simons Island 912-638-6732 or Brunswick 912-265-5292.

ST. SIMONS ISLAND LIGHTHOUSE

(Beachview Drive, oceanfront)

St. Simons Island 31522

- Phone: (912) 638-4666
  Web: www.saintsimonslighthouse.org
- Hours: Monday-Saturday 10:00am-5:00pm, Sunday 1:30-5:00pm.
- Admission: $5.00 adult, $2.50 child (under 12).

This lighthouse is the oldest brick structure in the area and is still maintained as an operational light by the US Coast Guard. The 104-foot-tall lighthouse has 129 interior steps. It sits behind the lightkeeper's dwelling which now houses the Museum. The second floor of the lightkeepers building is set up just as it would be in 1800s. The best part of the site for families is the climb up the six flights of stairs to the top of the light for a look around. Great view! Notice that most lighthouses are made of brick but this one is mostly locally made tabby mixture.

ST. SIMONS TROLLEY TOUR

Pier on Mallery Street (The Village/Pier area)

St. Simons Island 31522

- Phone: (912) 638-0762, **Web: www.stsimonstours.com**
- Admission: $18.00 adult, $10.00 child (4-12).
- Tours: 11:00am and 1:00pm (mid-March through September), 1:00pm only (October through early March). Reservations or tickets in advance are not required, but arrive early for scheduled departures.

Tour historic St. Simons Island on an antique trolley. Start with this tour to orient the family and give clues to sites you'll want to visit during your stay. The humorous and delightful drive-by tour includes the lighthouse, Bloody

Marsh, Fort Frederica, Retreat Plantation (where relics from slavery days still exist), and a walking tour of Christ Church (what famous Presidents have attended church here?) Hear stories about the slave family that owns the best property on the Island (Neptune). What is tabby? Do you hear footsteps from Frederic the Friendly ghost when walking up the lighthouse stairs? What is the #1 food produced by the marshes? Why is Spanish moss not Spanish? Nor, is it something you would want to bag up and take home. It's possible, when looking closely at certain of the oak trees that cover the island, to find one actually looking back at you. These are the Tree Spirits-lovingly carved faces emerging from the trees. Your tour guide will point some out to you. The images portray the sailors who lost their lives at sea aboard the sailing ships that were once made from St. Simons Island oak. Their sad, sorrowful expressions seem to reflect the grieving appearance of the trees themselves with their drooping branches and moss.

CAPTAIN MIKE'S DOLPHIN ADVENTURE

1 Old US 80 East (Lazaretto Creek Marina just before or after the Lazaretto Bridge, follow Marina signs)

Tybee Island 31328

- Phone: (912) 786-5848 or (800) 242-0166
  Web: www.tybeedolphins.com
- Admission: $12.00 adult, $5.00 child (12 and under)
- Tours: Call for daily, seasonal schedule. Usually twice daily during warm weather.
- Miscellaneous: The boat used is a working fishing boat, too. Metal seat ledges are around the perimeter of the boat and it is mostly covered by a canopy. However, because it is not a pontoon boat, you may experience sea sickness if you're prone to that. Just avoid moving to the front of the boat and you should be fine.

Looking for dolphin is just part of this cruise (you'll see dozens). Spot their blow holes (don't you love the "snorts") and then you'll see each special mammal fin (every dolphin's is different). Kids yell at the sight of every one, especially the ones closest to the boat! Do you know how long a baby dolphin (calf) stays with its mother? How do dolphins sleep? Besides the great exposure to dolphins, you'll learn lots about the lighthouse, Fort, shrimp boats and pelicans. If you love a narrated, learning tour about dolphins and their environment, this is an excellent tour.

FORT PULASKI NATIONAL MONUMENT

(US 80, 2 miles before reaching Tybee)

Tybee Island 31328

- Phone: (912) 786-5787, **Web: www.nps.gov/fopu**
- Hours: Daily 9:00am-7:00pm (summer). Daily 9:00am-5:00pm (rest of year).
- Admission: $3.00 per adult (age 17+). Children are FREE.

This fort was built between 1829 on Cockspur Island to guard the sea approach to Savannah. Future Confederate General Robert E. Lee was assigned to the fort as an engineer. When the Confederates seized Fort Pulaski in 1861, they thought the brick fort would be an impregnable blockade. However, the use of new rifled cannons forced their surrender in just over one day's bombardment. After this, forts of this type were obsolete. Scenic marshlands and uplands, towering walls, artillery tunnels, two moats and a wide drawbridge are special features. Later, the fort was used as part of the Underground Railroad. It was even the site of baseball games. As you visit, be mindful of safety. Recommended activities include self-guided tours, fishing, hiking, picnicking and birding. As you cross the drawbridge, look for the jumping mullet fish (*too cool!*).

TYBEE ISLAND LIGHTHOUSE

(US Hwy 80 at Fort Screven, follow signs)

Tybee Island 31328

- Phone: (912) 786-5801 **Web: www.tybeelighthouse.org**
- Hours: Daily 9:00am-5:30pm. Closed Tuesdays.
- Admission: $6.00 adult, $5.00 senior (62+) & child (6-17).

Visitors can climb 178 steps to the top of America's third oldest and Georgia's oldest lighthouse that is still working today and recently restored. Enjoy a spectacular view of the entire island, then visit the keeper's cottage. The cottage appears as if the keeper and family have just left for a moment. The museum features exhibits of early life on the Island, Indian and Civil War weaponry and dolls. By the way, when you finish climbing up and down the 178 steps, you are awarded a certificate saying so!

TYBEE ISLAND MARINE SCIENCE CENTER

1510 Strand Avenue (by Tybee Island pier and pavilion)

Tybee Island 31328

- Phone: (912) 786-5917, **Web: www.tybeemsc.org**
- Hours: Daily 9:00am-5:00pm.
- Admission: $4.00 adult, $3.00 child (3-16). Add $3.00 for beach walks with guides.

The museum consists of aquariums and a touch tank containing specimens indigenous to the coast of Georgia. Exhibits provide information on shells, sharks, marine mammals, sea turtles, marine mammals, marine pollution, the salt marsh, a cross-section of the beach, and maritime forest. Discovery beach walks and seinings are conducted daily. Help pull the seine net and experience the thrill of the catch. Examine the catch and learn why the objects are different or similar to other coastal catches. Besides the interesting beach walks, our favorite part was the touch tank.

Baby crabs, stingrays and living sand dollars were all there to touch. We were afraid to touch some of them so we asked a guide to help. It's surprising how much you can use all of your senses inside and outside the facility.

OBEDIAH'S OKEFENOK

5115 Swamp Road (US 82 onto Gilmore Street, follow signs about 8.5 miles south of town)

Waycross 31502

- Phone: (912) 287-0090, **Web: www.okefenokeeswamp.com**
- Hours: Daily 10:00am-5:00pm.
- Admission: $3.00-$4.50 (age 6+).

Mr. Barber was born in July of 1825, married three times and fathered twenty children. In the mid-1800s, Obediah constructed a one-story cabin with wooded pegged walls and puncheon floors on the northern border of the Okefenokee Swamp. He and his father Isaac were said to be the first white settlers in the area. Legend has it that Obediah killed a large black bear with a fat knot tree branch. A colorful character and man of great honor and integrity, along with a physical structure of over 6 1/2 feet, Obediah was also called the "Southeast Paul Bunyan." Take the elevated boardwalk and trails past the cabins and wildlife. Meet an alligator, python, giant ostrich, black bear, cougar and an assortment of unusual spiders. See dioramas of action scenes from the swamp. The Homestead consists of buildings and exhibits that have been restored as an example of the lifestyle in the area in the mid 1800s to early 1900s. Count how many beds are in the house.

OKEFENOKEE SWAMP PARK

(7 miles south of town, off US 1, off US 82, follow signs)

Waycross 31502

- Phone: (912) 283-4056, **Web: www.okeswamp.com**
- Hours: Daily 9:00am-5:30pm.
- Admission: $12.00 adult, $11.00 senior (62+), Military or child (5-11). Add $4.00 for boat tour (1/2 hour long).
- Miscellaneous: Parents and grandparents may remember the Walt Kelly comic strip - "POGO" possum and his Okefenoke swamp friends. Several areas of the park are dedicated to this.

Often perceived as a deep, dark, scary place, this wonder world of the Okefenokee is a preserved segment of what was here when America began. Boat tours are offered on original Indian waterways. See Pioneer Island and native animals in their own habitat or Pioneer Homestead, Honey Bee Farm, Turpentine Site or Seminole Indian Village. Enjoy productions and concerts in the amphitheater. The Wildlife Show, scheduled for different times during the day, is a huge hit with the kids. The host will bring out baby alligators, snakes and other wildlife, and give a short lecture on wildlife at this park. The train ride is also a delight. Learn about the natives - both human and plant or animal. They actually name the alligators here and you'll meet some that come along out of the water over towards the train to say hello! You'll come even closer to the gators in the boat tour. They're so sad when they find out you're not gonna feed them! (or be fed!) Stop at Pioneer Island and walk around a typical homestead and general store. This entire site is unique and cute - and, we promise - there will be lots of gators!

LAURA S. WALKER STATE PARK

5653 Laura Walker Road (9 miles southeast of Waycross on GA 177)

Waycross 31503

- Phone: (912) 287-4900, **Web: www.gastateparks.org**
- Hours: Daily 7:00am-10:00pm.
- Admission: FREE

This 63-acre park is one of the few state parks ever named for a woman, and richly deserved. Laura Walker was a Georgia writer, teacher, civic leader and naturalist who was a great lover of trees and worked for their preservation. Located near the Okefenokee Swamp, the park is home to many fascinating creatures and plants, including alligators. Walking along the lake shore and nature trail, visitors may see carnivorous pitcher plants, the shy gopher tortoise, numerous oak varieties, owls and great blue herons. Facilities at the park include tent and trailer sites, picnic shelters, a swimming pool, group camping, fishing, boating, canoeing, water-skiing and swimming.

OKEFENOKEE HERITAGE CENTER

1460 N. Augusta Avenue

Waycross 31503

- Phone: (912) 285-4260, **Web: www.okeheritage.org**
- Hours: Tuesday-Saturday 10:00am-4:30pm.
- Admission: $2.00-$3.00 per person.

The story of the heritage and life of people who lived in and around the Okefenokee Swamp and Native American life in South Georgia are documented through artifacts and exhibits. Outdoor exhibits to explore include a 1911 Baldwin Steam Locomotive and tender with additional cars, the Waycross Journal (a 1900s print shop) and the General Thomas Hilliard house, an 1840s farmhouse and outbuildings and varying art exhibits.

SOUTHERN FOREST WORLD

1440 N. Augusta Avenue, **Waycross** 31503

- Phone: (912) 285-4056
- Hours: Tuesday-Saturday 9:00am-5:00pm.
- Admission: $2.00 per person.

Adjacent to the Okefenokee Heritage Center, Southern Forest World features forestry exhibits documenting the importance of the development of forestry in the South. Fun and educational with hands-on exhibits, trees to climb, a collection of logging tools and a nature trail to explore. Stuckie the Dog, a canine that got caught in a hollow tree and mummified over 40 years ago, is here too.

SUGGESTED LODGING AND DINING

VILLAS BY THE SEA RESORT HOTEL - **Jekyll Island**, 1175 N Beachview Drive, (912) 635-2521 or (800) 841-6262 or **www.jekyllislandga.com**. Lovely villas with fully equipped kitchens, private living room/dining areas full baths, separate bedroom(s) and private patio or balcony. 1,2, or 3-bedroom villas nestled among 17 acres of stately oaks with a partially shaded large pool area and 2,000 feet of oceanside beach. Restaurant with early bird specials and a Kids Menu. Other amenities include bicycle rentals for Jekyll's 20 miles of scenic paved trails, playground, volleyball, badminton, and basketball. $100.00-$200.00 per night. Lower rates available for mid-week and weekly stays.

BLUE HERON BED & BREAKFAST - **Meridian**, 1 Blue Heron Lane (I-95 exit 58, GA 99 southeast towards Sapelo Island ferry, 1 1/2 mile before ferry, left on Sea Breeze Drive). (912) 437-4304 or **www.blueheroninngacoast.com**. Wanna spend the overnight on a real marsh (teaming with shrimp, blue crab, blue heron, egrets and maybe an alligator or snake)? Most all the rooms are facing the marsh, with private balconies. A luscious freshly prepared gourmet breakfast (their signature lime french toast - or plain for the kids) is part of your stay. Bill and Jan are gracious hosts and the modern home is minutes away from the ferry over to Sapelo Island where you can tour the remote island (see separate listing). Have a boat? The owners say families can stay for days if they bring water transportation. Nice combo for adventuresome families. Great comfy hospitality inside, yet wildlife galore outside. Rates $85-130.00/night.

<u>COMFORT SUITES HISTORIC DISTRICT</u> - **Savannah**, 630 West Bay Street (under bridge). (912) 629-2001 or **www.comfortsuites.com/hotel/ga323.com**. Located within walking distance of the historic area including River Street and City Market, each spacious suite has a microwave and frig. There is also a heated indoor pool, spa and complimentary deluxe continental breakfast.

<u>BARBARA JEAN'S RESTAURANT</u> - **St. Simons Island**, 214 Mallery Street (Village), (912) 634-6500 or **www.barbara-jeans.com**. Famous for "Eastern shore" crab cakes (best ever) and home-style entrees (like meatloaf) with southern style sides (greens, squash casserole). Open 11:00am-10:00pm daily. Kids Menu $3.00-$4.00.

<u>BEST WESTERN ISLAND INN</u> - **St. Simons Island**, 301 Main Street, Plantation Village (follow causeway straight on Demere, left into complex), **www.bestwesternstsimons.com** or (912) 638-7805. Enjoy the sub-tropical landscaping around the outdoor pool or unwind in the bubbling hot tub beneath the gazebo. They have a complimentary deluxe continental breakfast bar and bike rentals on site.

<u>MULLET BAY RESTAURANT</u> - **St. Simons Island**, 512 Ocean Boulevard, **www.mulletbayrestaurant.com**. (912) 638-0703. Seafood (esp. their fish of the day), steaks, sandwiches, chicken, burgers, po-boys. Kids (and parents) can crayon on the table cloth. Kids menu (under $5.00). Casual dining, moderate prices, dining indoors and outdoors.

FANNIES' ON THE BEACH RESTAURANT - **Tybee Island**, on the Strand near 17th Street oceanside. (912) 786-6109. Right near our favorite spot (left or right of the pier) on our favorite Georgia beach, Tybee Beach, is a fun beach restaurant. Look for the sign near the pavilion that says "Time to Eat". Order anything with shrimp or a pizza and you will be happy. Try to sit upstairs on the deck or the real boat! Live music most nights - specializing in "Marsh-grass" musical blend of blues, bluegrass and low country.

WHISTLE STOP CAFÉ - **Savannah**, (912) 238-1779. At the far end of the Visitors Center station building, it serves breakfast and lunch in a railroad car setting. Average menu pricing $4.00-$6.00. Kiddies Caboose Menu has choices of Freightliner Fish, Southbound Spaghetti, Central Georgia Chicken Fingers, or Hobo Beef Stew.

Chapter 6
South West Area - (SW)

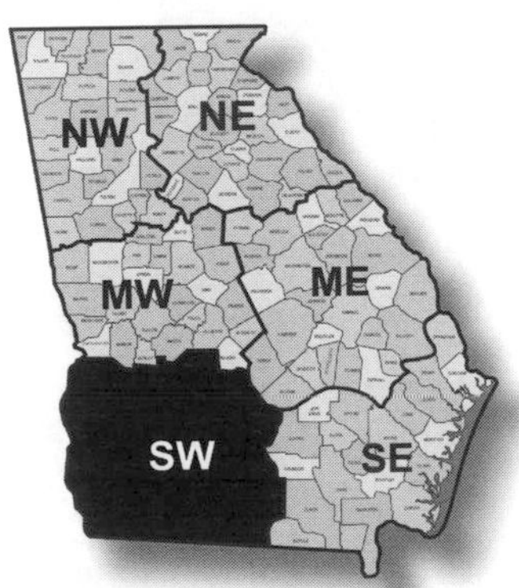

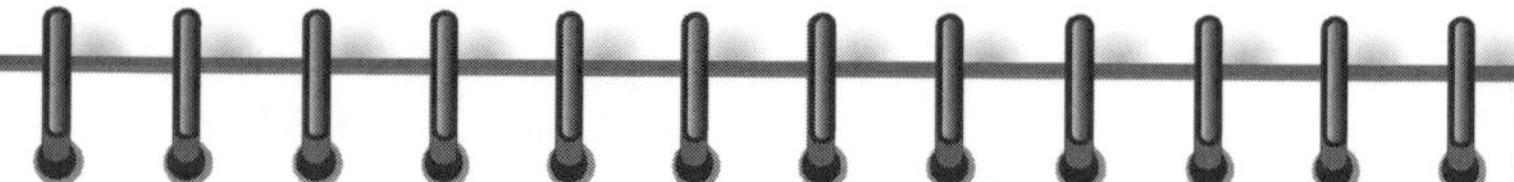

Our Favorites...

* Habitat for Humanity Global Village - Americus

* Georgia Veterans State Park (Lake Blackshear Resort) - Cordele

* SAM Shortline Excursion Train - Cordele

* Jimmy Carter National Historic Site - Plains

All Aboard - the SAM Shortline

REED BINGHAM STATE PARK

542 Reed Bingham Road (6 miles west of town on GA 37 via I-75 exit 39 and 14 miles east of US 319 in Moultrie), **Adel** 31620

- Phone: (229) 896-3551, **Web: www.gastateparks.org**
- Hours: Daily 7:00am-10:00pm.
- Admission: FREE. Fee for camping.

The park has become a major boating and waterskiing attraction in south Georgia. The Coastal Plain Nature Trail and Gopher Tortoise Nature Trail wind through a cypress swamp, sandhill area and other habitats representative of southern Georgia. Watchful visitors may see waterfowl, the threatened gopher turtles and indigo snake, and other creatures. However, the park's most famous residents are the thousands of black vultures and turkey vultures that arrive in late November and stay through early April. Other recreation opportunities include a swimming beach and mini-golf.

PARKS AT CHEHAW

105 Chehaw Park Road, **Albany** 31701

- Phone: (229) 430-5277, **Web: www.parksatchehaw.org**
- Hours: Daily 9:00am-5:00pm. Closed Thanksgiving, Christmas and New Years.
- Admission: $4.00-$6.00 (age 3+) for zoo and park.

Walk through Georgia's flourishing forests inhabited by its native creatures. Travel down the creeks, streams, and trails that were traveled by the Native Americans of this area. Watch the white-tailed deer, raccoons, squirrels, and birds of all kinds as they play in their natural habitat. A basic zoo adds flare with Free Ranging Lemurs, Ben's Barnyard & Children's Farm, Giant Tortoises, American Bison, and a Swampland with alligators. A train takes visitors on a 20-minute ride through the park and the adjacent natural restoration area.

THRONATEESKA HERITAGE CENTER

100 W. Roosevelt Avenue (Heritage Plaza)

Albany 31701

- Phone: (229) 432-6955, **Web: www.heritagecenter.org**
- Hours: Thursday-Saturday Noon-4:00pm. Planetarium Showtimes and Discovery Center Thursday-Friday 2:45pm, Saturdays 12:30pm, 1:30pm, 2:30pm.
- Admission: $3.25-$4.25 (age 6+).

The Discovery Center is a place to find out about science with your hands, ears and eyes. At Imagination Stations, visitors learn about light and electricity, magnetism and sound, nature and history. It's a hands-on experience to awaken scientific curiosity about your world. The Model Train Exhibit is located directly behind steam locomotive Georgia Northern 107 (you can't miss it) and housed in an actual railroad baggage car (Southern Railway 518). This detailed exhibit depicts a train journey from the city to the country. In the Wetherbee Planetarium it's always a starry, starry night. With a wide variety of programs from Diamonds in the Sky to a Report from Venus. Good facility for locals to share hands-on science and history with students.

ALBANY MUSEUM OF ART

311 Meadowlark Drive (I-75 south, right on GA 300. GA 234 west and finally north on Meadowlark)

Albany 31707

- Phone: (229) 439-8400, **Web: www.albanymuseum.com**
- Hours: Tuesday-Saturday 10:00am-5:00pm, Sunday 1:00-4:00pm.
- Admission: $4.00 adult, $2.00 senior and child. Sundays are FREE.

Join them for Family Days- a child friendly guided tour of one of the current exhibitions. Then spend time working together to create your own masterpiece based on the artwork you have seen. Before you leave, don't forget to explore AMAzing Space. AMAzing Space is the Albany Museum of Art's interactive hands-on gallery designed with children in mind. There are five sections to AMAzing Space which are based on the Permanent Collection of African, American and European art. Every visit, be sure to check out the latest in the Learning Curve gallery displaying the artwork of children and adults who are current students of art classes and schoolrooms.

HABITAT FOR HUMANITY GLOBAL VILLAGE & DISCOVERY CENTER

721 West Church Street (I-75 to US 280 heading west, follow signs)

Americus 31709

- Phone: (229) 924-0577 or (866) 924-5823
  Web: www.habitat.org/gvdc/
- Hours: Tuesday-Saturday 9:00am-5:00pm, Closed Thanksgiving, Christmas and New Year's Day. Open for group tours daily.
- Admission: $5.00 adult, $4.00 senior, $3.00 student (over 6).

Habitat for Humanity International is a Christian ministry dedicated to eliminating poverty housing. Founded in 1976 by Millard & Linda Fuller, Habitat for Humanity International and its affiliates in more than 3,000 communities, in 92 nations, have built and sold more than 150,000 homes to partner families with no-profit, zero-interest mortgages. Begin your visit viewing a Photo Gallery of the Habitat story in pictures and watch film shorts highlighting Habitat's worldwide work. Now, with your Global Village Passport in hand, begin walking through the "Living in Poverty" houses. These are re-created structures normally found in severely poor areas of the world. Why do some dwellings have a single light bulb hanging from the ceiling when they don't even have electricity? Most Americans will never leave our country and visit third world countries…this may be their only exposure. Now, on to more hopeful settings: the Global Village of 35 houses built to provide better environmentally and culturally appropriate housing. At each house, review your passport for info on the building materials used and the style of life of the inhabitants. Kids engage by placing a stamp in their passport as proof they have visited each home. While touring houses, stop at one of the demonstration centers and learn how bricks, tile and other building materials are made and used in construction. Then, try your hand at making compressed-earth blocks or roof tile. This site so touched us and educated us that we recommend it to every family as a "must see" attraction!

CRIME AND PUNISHMENT MUSEUM & LAST MEAL CAFÉ

241 East College Avenue (I-75 exit 82 west. Follow signs to downtown)

Ashburn 31714

- Phone: (800) 471-9696, **Web: www.jailmuseum.com**
- Hours: Tuesday-Saturday 10:00am-5:00pm. Café open 11:00am-2:00pm.
- Admission: $1.00-$3.00.

Built in 1906, the Turner County Jail resembles a castle outside, but not inside. The original jail cells remain upstairs, the sheriff's family quarters downstairs. Although mature for children, you can see the death cell, Old Sparky electrocution chair, and trap door for hangings. Combine this with heart wrenching stories about infamous criminals, murders, hangings, ghosts and even a love story. Check out the striped prisoner clothes. After the tour, stop in for dessert "to die for" at the Last Meal Café. There is a long standing tradition of death row inmates requesting their last meal with a lavish dessert. Enjoy Southern cobbler, pie, cake or ice cream or full meals are available for groups with advance reservations. Clever theme.

WORLD'S LARGEST PEANUT

(off I-75), **Ashburn** 31714

- Phone: (229) 567-9696

Clearly seen beside Interstate 75, this monument is the largest of its kind in the nation. It is a daily reminder of the fact that Georgia's number one cash crop is peanuts. The peanut is approximately 20 feet tall!

KOLOMOKI MOUNDS STATE HISTORIC PARK

205 Indian Mounds Road (6 miles north of town off US 27)

Blakely 39823

- Phone: (229) 724-2150, **Web: www.gastateparks.org**
- Hours: Park, Daily 7:00am-10:00pm. Museum, Daily 8:00am-5:00pm.
- Admission: $1.50-$2.50 per person.

This unusual park is an important archaeological site as well as a scenic recreational area. Seven earthen mounds within the park were built over 1000 -2000 years ago by the Swift Creek and Weeden Island Indians. The mounds include the oldest state great temple mound, two burial mounds and four ceremonial mounds. When you walk into the museum, you're walking inside a partially excavated mound, providing an unusual setting for viewing artifacts and a film. Outdoor activities include camping, fishing, pedal boat and canoe rental, swimming pool, mini-golf, and 5 miles of hiking trails.

SWAMP GRAVY

166 East Main Street (Cotton Hall)

Colquitt 39817

- Phone: (229) 758-5450, **Web: www.swampgravy.com**
- Hours: Thursday - Saturday 7:30pm, Sundays 3:00pm.
- Admission: Thursdays $22.00; Friday, Saturday & Sunday $25.00.
- Miscellaneous: The town's visual narrative, "We've Got a Story to Tell", showcases nine murals in Town Square & throughout town.

The folk life play Swamp Gravy, while steeped in Southern tradition, presents universal stories about life and death, family and community. Each performance is a blend of comedy, drama, and music featuring a cast of more than 100 volunteers. All of Swamp Gravy's plays are based on real life stories, taken from taped interviews and adapted for the stage. The state's general assembly designated Swamp Gravy as the "Official Folk Life Play of Georgia". Located inside a 60-year-old renovated cotton warehouse now aptly known as Cotton Hall, the hall itself is a tourist attraction. In addition to its theater, Cotton Hall houses a gift shop, the Museum of Southern Cultures, and a Commons area. Experience the play that "...united a town and moved a nation."

GEORGIA VETERANS MEMORIAL STATE PARK

2459A US 280 West (I-75 exit 101west to Cordele on US 280)

Cordele 31015

- Phone: (229) 276-2371, **Web: www.gastateparks.org**
- Hours: Daily 7:00am-10:00pm.

Established as a memorial to U.S. veterans, this park features a museum with aircraft, armored vehicles, uniforms, weapons, medals and other items from the Revolutionary

War through the Gulf War. Kids gravitate to the outdoor exhibit of real-life wartime tanks and aircraft. We even found a floating tank. They all seem so large to kids. The SAM Shortline Excursion Train runs through the park on its way from Cordele to Plains. Modern camping sites, rental cottages, R/C Model Airplane Flying Field, a seasonal swimming pool and beach, a marina and one-mile Nature Trail add to the site. An 18-hole golf course and pro shop, along with 8,600-acre Lake Blackshear, make this one of Georgia's most popular state parks.

S A M SHORTLINE EXCURSION TRAIN

105 East 9th Avenue (I-75, take exit 101/Hwy 280 west to Hwy 41. You may also board the train at any of the stops), **Cordele** 31015

- Phone: (229) 276-2715 or (877) 427-2457
  Web: www.samshortline.com
- Admission: Coach Class - Seats are not assigned: $21.95 adult, $18.95 senior (62+) & veterans, $11.95 child (3-12). Premium -has tables and chairs, ceiling fans and carpet. Tables may be assigned: $28.95 adult, $16.95 child. Walk-up from Americus to Plains: $12.00-$23.00 adult, $7.00-$12.00 child.
- Tours: Reservations: 800-864-7275. Walk-ups: first come, first serve. All departures from Cordele at 9:30am, returning around 5:00pm. See online schedule or brochure for Thursday, Friday, Saturday and Monday departures (July - December).
- Miscellaneous: Please note FLIPS FLOPS and sandals without backs are not allowed on the train for safety purposes. Rain gear is suggested since most depots are not covered and the train runs rain-or-shine. Hot dogs, sausage dogs and BBQ sandwiches are available on the train. Drinks, ice cream, chips and hot popcorn, plus numerous souvenirs, are ready for you to purchase in the Leslie Car aboard the train. Some towns have restaurants, but riders with special dietary needs may want to pack a picnic lunch.

S A M Shortline Excursion Train *(cont.)*

Climb aboard the air-conditioned vintage train traveling past pecan groves and scenic country farms, stopping in four towns filled with historic attractions, restaurants and shopping. Most tours stop for 45 minutes to 75 minutes at each town. While you can board the Southwest Georgia's Excursion Train at any of its stops, the official beginning is at Cordele. The first stop on the route is Georgia Veterans State Park, one of Georgia's most-visited state parks, featuring sparkling Lake Blackshear and fascinating military exhibits (see separate listing). Your next stop may be Leslie, home of the Rural Telephone Museum that showcases antiques, switchboards, classic cars, colorful murals – and, of course, antique telephones ($3.00 adults and $1.00 students). The Victorian town of Americus is your next stop. Tour Habitat for Humanity's new Global Village (see separate listing). The small Georgia town made famous by President Jimmy Carter is your next stop. While in Plains, browse President Carter's campaign museum, then buy a bag of peanuts from local merchants. A bit further down the tracks is the community of Archery, featuring the president's boyhood home. The train will stop just steps from his old front porch, and you'll have plenty of time to explore the farm before the SAM Shortline returns to Cordele. Because this all day trip makes so many stops and allows you to tour the highlights of the area - it is the idea way to tour with kids. This is, by far, one of the best overall train rides we've ever experienced! All aboard!

SEMINOLE STATE PARK

7870 State Park Road (16 miles south of town via GA 39 or 23 miles west of Bainbridge on GA 253)

Donalsonville 39845

- Phone: (229) 861-3137, **Web: www.gastateparks.org**
- Hours: Daily 7:00am-10:00pm.
- Admission: FREE. Fee for camping and cottages.

Lake Seminole, a 37,500-acre reservoir known for excellent sport fishing and boating. The lake is shallow, but natural lime sink ponds have left areas of cool, clear water with a variety of fish. The threatened gopher tortoise, Georgia's state reptile, makes its home along the nature trail (2.2 miles long) designed to interpret the wiregrass community habitat. Cottages and many campsites are situated on the water's edge, offering excellent lake views. The park offers bicycle and canoe rentals.

BLUE AND GRAY MUSEUM

116 N. Johnston Street (I-75 exit 82 east on Hwy 107 for 22 miles)

Fitzgerald 31750

- Phone: (229) 426-5069
  Web: www.fitzgeraldga.org/Blue&GrayMuseum.htm
- Hours: Tuesday-Saturday 10:00am-4:00pm, Sunday 1:00-5:00pm.
- Admission: $1.00-$3.00 per person.

There's a remarkable harmony story in Fitzgerald. Experience the history yourself in this town created by Yanks and Rebs, former enemies, working together after the Civil War. See the story revealed in the museum. Watch the "Marching as One" video documentary - the whole story of how an attorney created a plan to carve a city out of the woods for aging Union Veterans - and how enemies finally became friends. Housed in a historic depot, the site is full of rare

Civil War artifacts from both sides of the conflict - each telling a story. See reunion caps worn by Republic and Confederates and the stories behind each soldier. Who received the Congressional Medal of Honor and who received the Southern Cross of Honor? Extend your visit by walking around town. Visit Evergreen Cemetery and find Yanks and Rebs "resting side by side". How did one man from Indiana truly create a peaceful community?

BOWENS MILL FISH HATCHERY

1773 Bowens Mill Hwy (US 129 north of town)

Fitzgerald 31750

- Phone: (229) 426-5035
- Hours: Monday-Friday 8:00am-4:30pm.
- Admission: FREE
- Tours: 45 minute tour of how a fish hatchery operates. Minimum two day notice.

Tours of this state fish hatchery include largemouth bass, catfish, bluegill and red-ear sunfish. Fish are raised from "babies" here and released to state lakes and ponds for abundant fishing in Georgia.

JEFFERSON DAVIS MEMORIAL

338 Jeff Davis Park Road (I-75 exit 78 east on GA 32 to Irwinville. Turn left into park), **Fitzgerald** 31750

- Phone: (229) 831-2335, **Web: www.gastateparks.org**
- Hours: Tuesday-Saturday 9:00am-5:00pm, Sunday 2:00-5:30pm. Closed Mondays except holidays.
- Admission: $1.50-$2.50 per person.

When Confederate President Jefferson Davis and a few remaining staff members crossed the Savannah River into Georgia, they didn't know that pursuit was so close behind. At dawn, they were surrounded by two independent groups of Union cavalry who were unaware of each other's presence. Gunfire continued until the federal forces realized they had been shooting at one another. Davis was taken prisoner and held in Virginia for two years until released. Today, a monument marks the sport where he was arrested. Visitors can tour the historic site that includes a museum, short trail and picnic facilities.

GEORGE T. BAGBY STATE PARK AND LODGE

Route 1, Box 201 (4 miles north of Fort Gaines off GA 39)

Fort Gaines 39851

- Phone: (229) 768-2571
  Web: www.georgebagbylodgepark.org
- Hours: Daily 7:00am-10:00pm.
- Admission: FREE. Fee for lodge and cottages.

This resort park features a 60-room lodge, restaurant, swimming pool, cottages and golf course. The park's marina and boat ramp offer easy access to the lake for fishing and boating. A three-mile nature trail winds through hardwoods and pines. There are also canoe, fishing boat & pontoon boat rentals.

PROVIDENCE CANYON STATE CONSERVATION PARK

Route 1, Box 158 (7 miles west of Lumpkin on GA 39C)

Lumpkin 31815

- Phone: (229) 838-6202, **Web: www.gastateparks.org**
- Hours: Daily 7:00am - dark.
- Admission: FREE. Fee for camping.

This is Georgia's "Little Grand Canyon" where rare Plumleaf Azalea and other wildflowers (and pink, orange, red an purple hues of canyon soil) make a beautiful natural full-color picture. Enjoy views of the canyons from the rim trail.

Camping is available. An interpretive center explains how the massive gullies (the deepest being 150 feet) were caused by erosion due to poor farming practices in the 1800s.

WESTVILLE

1 MLK Drive (US 27 & SR 27)

Lumpkin 31815

- Phone: (229) 838-6410, **Web: www.westville.org**
- Hours: Tuesday-Saturday 10:00am-5:00pm, Sunday 1:00-5:00pm. Closed major winter holidays.
- Admission: $10.00 adult, $8.00 senior & military, $4.00 child (K-12)
- Miscellaneous: Like lots of action going on? Check out their seasonal events (see listings in the last chapter).

The hard-working townspeople here have replicated a working village of year 1850, complete with appropriate gardens, furnishings, and dirt streets. They make cotton cloth at Westville just as they did in 1850. Some of the houses at Westville have curtains and quilts made from cloth right here in the town. A girl usually learned to quilt by the time she was eight or nine. Cloth wasn't plentiful, so quilts were fashioned from bits and pieces of scrap cloth sewn together. In rural 1850 Georgia, very few families owned wood stoves. Meals were cooked over open fires. Sample their homemade gingerbread cooked on a wood stove. They dip wax candles (made from beeswax or animal fat) at Westville, weather permitting. You'll find the shops of a blacksmith, potter, boot maker and cabinet maker, as well as a general store and doctor's office. Step inside an old church and sit on the handmade pews. The volunteers at the schoolhouse will be glad to tell you all about learning before the Civil War.

SOUND PLAY

108 Railroad Street, **Parrott** 31777

- Phone: (229) 623-5545, **Web: www.soundplay.com**
- Hours: Weekdays 10:00am-6:00pm and some weekend hours. Informal visitors are always welcome.
- Admission: FREE
- Tours: They are happy to have visitors and can accommodate tours or mini-workshops/demos if given enough notice.

Visitors are encouraged to tour the workshop and play drums shaped like box turtles or alligators, metallophones, and other unusual outdoor musical instruments that are made on-site. Using recycled and "tuned" wood and metal materials, Bond Anderson creates and operates a busy commercial enterprise here. They usually have a variety of instruments waiting to be installed for visitors to play as a "test run". Look for their works of musical art at outdoor science centers and gardens for kids. This idea is a great way to expose your family to the art of physics and music interplay.

JIMMY CARTER NATIONAL HISTORIC SITE

300 North Bond Street (places throughout downtown and along railroad tracks)

Plains 31780

- Phone: (229) 824-4104, **Web: www.nps.gov/jica**
- Hours: Most buildings open at 9:00am or 10:00am, closing at 4:30-5:00pm.
- Admission: FREE
- Miscellaneous: An orientation film is shown in the visitor center auditorium and a self-guided tour book is available for purchase at the visitor center. Daily each June-October: Exhibits outside and inside the buildings give the visitor and idea of what life was like for Jimmy Carter on the farm.

Jimmy Carter National Historic Site *(cont.)*

Dedicated to the 39th President of the United States, this national park site includes President Jimmy Carter's residence, boyhood farm, the railroad depot which served as his campaign headquarters during the 1976 election, and the Plains High School Museum & Welcome Center filled with Carter memorabilia. Few U.S. Presidents have had such close ties with where they were born and raised. The rural southern culture of Plains, Georgia, that revolves around farming, church and school, had a large influence in molding the character and in shaping the political policies of the 39th President of the United States. The town slogan "Plains, Peanuts and A President" is personified here. PLAINS DEPOT (Main Street and M.L. Hudson Street) - The building was restored as Jimmy Carter's 1976 campaign headquarters. Visitors may view different exhibits and films on Carter's 1976 presidential campaign. CARTER BOYHOOD HOME - Old Plains Highway, Archery - Exhibits outside and inside the buildings give the visitor an idea of what life was like for Jimmy Carter on the farm. Listen to Jimmy talking about each room. Why couldn't the family ever finish a meal without interruption? What were some of young Jimmy's favorite boyhood treasures?

SWEET GRASS DAIRY

19635 US Hwy 19N (I-75 south to exit 62, Tifton. Follow Rte. 319 south. Turn right on US 19 for 5 miles), **Thomasville** 31792

- Phone: (229) 227-0752, **Web: www.sweetgrassdairy.com**
- Tours: By appointment only. Scheduled tours on Thursday, Fridays, and Saturdays. $5.00 per person (age 3+). Minimum 15 people per tour. They will not schedule any tours in November, December or January. They cannot guarantee they will be making cheese during the tour as the cheese making schedule varies.

- Miscellaneous: If you have less than 15 people, we encourage you to come out to one of Market Days on the farm where they give tours all days, and have a big cheese tasting and animal petting area.

Sweet Grass practices biologically sustainable, grass-based farming. The Jersey cow and multi-breed goat herds are rotationally grazed and live their entire lives outside, roaming lush pastures and browsing the South Georgia woods. Tours start around 8:30am because the goats finish milking around 9:00am. The tour is broken up into three parts. First, you will see the milking parlor and the goats being milked. Secondly, you will see the cheese making area as well as taste a cheese sampling of several different types of Dairy cheese. Lastly, you will spend some time with the animals in the field (this is usually everybody's favorite part since goats are as friendly as dogs). The tour lasts anywhere from an hour to an hour and a half depending on how many questions the group has. The best time of year to come is March, April and May because they have many baby goats, lambs, and piglets. Try Georgia Pecan Chevre (goat cheese) - a Southern Georgia fresh product.

AGRIRAMA

P O Box Q (I-75, Exit 63B), **Tifton** 31793

- Phone: (229) 386-3344 or (800) 767-1875 **www.agrirama.com**
- Hours: Tuesday-Saturday 9:00am-5:00pm. Also closed on New Year's Day, Thanksgiving Day, three days prior to Christmas and Christmas Day.
- Admission: $7.00 adult, $6.00 senior (55+), $4.00 child (5-16).
- Miscellaneous: Enjoy the Wiregrass Opry on selected Saturday nights.

Agrirama *(cont.)*

The State's living history museum consists of four distinct areas: traditional farm community of the 1870s, progressive farmstead of the 1890s, industrial sites complex, and a rural town. Costumed interpreters are on location daily to explain and demonstrate the lifestyle and activities of the period. See bacon and ham curing in the smoke-house and veggies preserved in the canning shed. Ride a logging train into the woods, walk down to the sawmill and turpentine still, see the cooper's shed and the blacksmith's shop before crossing the street to the working print shop. At the Feed and Seed Store and Drug Store, order your favorite refreshments from a working marble top soda fountain. Kids especially love Agrirama's barnyard animals. Because there are over 35 structures relocated to the site, you can meet many different tradesmen and crafters performing different chores. Be careful, they may ask you to help them.

NESPAL COASTAL PLAIN EXPERIMENT STATION

2356 Rainwater Road (I-75 exit 64, turn north on Hwy 41. Left on RDC Road, then left onto Moore Hwy, past the stoplight)

Tifton 31794

- Phone: (229) 386-7274, **Web: www.nespal.org**
- Hours: Monday-Friday 8:00am-5:00pm
- Admission: FREE
- Tours: By appointment. Pre-K and up. Best for age 10+

This facility is staffed by real scientists developing systems for environmentally and economically positive agriculture production. Programs for students include an Agricultural Awareness Day. Third and fourth grade students participate in this spring planting and fall harvesting project. Students learn the value of agriculture in their everyday lives as they plant and harvest Georgia's chief crops of peanuts, corn, and cotton. Students also learn about soil and water conservation, insects, and non-food products derived from agricultural crops. Other groups can plan visits according to their studies (ex. First graders learning the basic needs of simple plants).

WILD ADVENTURES THEME PARK

(I-75 exit 13)

Valdosta 31601

- Phone: (229) 219-7080, **Web: www.wildadventures.net**
- Hours: Open practically year-round at 10:00am. Closing time varies with season (6:00-10:00pm).
- Admission: $32.00-$39.00.

They boast five parks in one place. Through one gate there are wild rides, wild animals and wild entertainment...all with a safari animal theme. The park has 9 roller coasters, 5 water rides, go-karts, over 500 wild animals placed in natural habitats scattered throughout the park, and daily shows plus 50 big-name concerts and special events. Slide into something refreshing at Splash Island Water Park - ride Catchawave Bay or the Double Dip Zip, mist in the Rain Fortress or float Paradise River (seasonal weather-dependent hours). Entertaining shows feature animals, costumed characters, song, dance, magic and music. Board our safari train where you'll take a cross-continent ride through the open grasslands of Africa and Asia encountering elephants, antelope, zebra, giraffe and more. Walk through the Rain Forest on a journey through a natural wetland featuring birds, monkeys, reptiles and bears. Pet animals in the Wild West Petting Zoo. Evenings provide many eateries, a 3D laser and fireworks show and shopping along with numerous concerts.

ELLIS BROTHERS PECANS PACKING COMPANY

1315 Tippettville Road (I-75 exit 109 east)

Vienna 31092

- Phone: (229) 268-9041 or (800) 635-0616
  Web: www.werenuts.com
- Hours: Retail Store open 8:00am-7:00pm (including holidays).
- Tours: Guided tours by appointment.

Ellis Bros. Pecans is a family owned and operated wholesale and retail business. The original pecan grove was started in 1944 by Marvin and Irene Ellis. The shelling plant and retail store are located adjacent to the original pecan grove. Elliott Ellis and his sons manage the operation today. Ms. Irene continues to oversee her candy kitchen. Visitors can view the pecan-and peanut-packing process firsthand. Our favorite part - sampling! (and then buying a variety of products made on-site).

GEORGIA COTTON MUSEUM

1321 E. Union Street (I-75 exit 36)

Vienna 31092

- Phone: (229) 268-2045, **Web: www.historicvienna.org**
- Hours: Monday-Friday 9:00am-5:00pm, Saturday 9:00am-4:00pm.
- Admission: FREE

The history of cotton is told with the aid of farm tools, cotton bolls, a cotton bale, scale and planters desk that kept accurate records of the harvest. It includes the slave issues and how their participation in the production of cotton contributed to the economy. How did farmers deal with insects and poor weather? Ride through the county in the fall to see the beauty of "snow in the south" harvest. The cotton is so thick and so white that it appears to be snow on the ground.

SUGGESTED LODGING AND DINING

THE RETREAT AT LAKE BLACKSHEAR, **Cordele**, is a privately operated resort within Georgia Veterans State Park with 78 villa rooms, 10 cottages, indoor/outdoor pools and a restaurant. The sunsets are beautiful from your screened-in porch and folks around the pool tell us the boating is excellent, with friendly stations along the way to gas up or dock and grab some chow. Besides the nice pool area, the resort offers bicycle, paddle boat, canoe and kayak rentals. The golf course offers Jr. golf camps. This is a modern oasis in a natural setting. **www.lakeblackshearretreat.org**. (229) 276-1004 or average. $130-$140.00 per room/cabin (refrigerator in each room).

Chapter 7

Seasonal & Special Events

JANUARY

FDR'S BIRTHDAY CELEBRATION

MW – Warm Springs. Little White House Historic Site. (706) 655-5870. Celebrate the President's birthday with cake and tours. Admission. (January 30)

FEBRUARY

GROUNDHOG DAY CELEBRATION

NE – Lilburn, Yellow River Game Ranch. (877) 972-6643 or **www.yellowrivergameranch.com**. At Sunrise, each Groundhog Day, General Beau Lee, Georgia's Official Weather Prognosticator, peeks out to share or hide his shadow. Georgia's Secretary of State, proclaims the news in usually nippy weather. What food do they use to lure the animal out? Beau has a 93% rate of accuracy. The other one does not. (February 2)

GEORGIA HERITAGE CELEBRATIONS COLONIAL FAIRE AND MUSTER

SE – Savannah. Wormsloe Historic Site. (912) 651-2125. Military encampment, a Sutler's Row, crafts, demonstrations, and Colonial music. (February)

MARCH

ST. PATRICK'S DAY CELEBRATION

Musical concerts, Irish foods and a big morning parade. (St. Patrick's Day, March 17)

- ❑ **ME – Dublin**. Downtown. (478) 272-5546 or **www.dublin-georgia.com**
- ❑ **NE – Conyers**. Downtown. (800) 266-9377.

- **SE – Douglas**. Downtown. (912) 384-5161.
- **SE – Savannah**. City Market and River Street. (912) 273-4804.

RIVER BLAST

MW – Columbus. Port Columbus. (706) 327-9798 or **www.portcolumbus.org**. In 2004, the museum rolled out its newly restored scale model of the USS Monitor and let it fight a Confederate type ironclad ship in the Chattahoochee River. Sailors and marines from around the south show up to get combat training ala 1863, including serving on the big Brooke Rifled cannon over looking the river. (second weekend in March)

AZALEA STORYTELLING FESTIVAL

MW – LaGrange College. (706) 880-8276. Nationally acclaimed storytellers will visit LaGrange to spin comedic, nostalgic and moving tales at the annual Azalea Storytelling Festival. Admission (students half price). (first weekend in March)

CHERRY BLOSSOM FESTIVAL

MW – Macon. **www.cherryblossom.com** or (478) 751-7429. Events range from live animal shows to hot-air balloon festivals, parades, arts and crafts and live theatre productions to amusement rides, fireworks, historic tours and dances. Complimentary horse-drawn carriage rides and refreshments are also provided, including Cherries 'n Cream, an ice cream made specifically for the festival. Concerts held daily. Ninety percent of events are FREE. (ten days beginning mid-March)

March *(cont.)*

STITCHING STARS STORYTELLING FESTIVAL

NE – Athens. Seney-Stovall Chapel. (706) 613-3650 or **www.clarke.public.lib.ga.us/events/specialevents/stitching.html**. Share the wonderful art of storytelling with Northern Georgia. The name of our festival was inspired by the story-quilts of Harriet Powers, an African American quilter, born in captivity in Madison County, Georgia in 1837. Admission. (last Saturday in March)

CARIBFEST: CELEBRATION CARIBBEAN CULTURE

NW - Stone Mountain. Wade Walker Park. (866) 633-5252 or **www.caribfest.maccacentre.org**. Three days of culturally diverse visual arts, live performances, sports, games and authentic Caribbean food. (March)

SCOTTISH HERITAGE DAYS

SE – Darien. Fort King George State Historic Site. (912) 437-4770. In 1736, General James Oglethorpe brought a group of Scottish Highlanders to Georgia. In this event, they pay tribute to those brave Scots who settled Darien. A reenactment of the Battle of Bloody Marsh will be conducted along with other festivities related to Scottish culture and lifestyle. (last weekend in March)

POGOFEST

SE – Waycross. Okefenokee Swamp. (912) 283-3742 or **www.igopogo.com**. The festival honors Walt Kelly's 1950 Okefenokee Cartoon Character "POGO" Possum, with arts, crafts, a street dance and country music concert. Each year a nationally known Cartoonist is on hand to sign autographs and meet with cartoon enthusiasts. (last weekend in March)

FIRE ANT FESTIVAL

SW – Ashburn. Downtown (I-75 exit 82). (800) 471-9696. Known for its wacky and off the wall activities, the Festival offers family fun as they watch or participate in the fire ant calling contest, the fire ant fling and the fire ant surprise. Also, a drive-in movie, fireworks, bands, carnival and cooking contests with food. (fourth weekend in March)

APRIL (& EASTER EVENTS)

MOSSY CREEK BARNYARD FESTIVAL

MW – Perry-Warner Robins. Deep Piney Woods (6 miles east of I-75, exit 138, Thompson Road). (478) 922-8265 or **www.mossycreekfestival.com**. Step into an enchanted forest full of Appalachian mountain music, hammered dulcimer, folk songs, Fantasy Forest storytelling, and Ragtime piano. Watch wood-carving, weaving and hand-building fishing rods. There is also animal petting areas and hayrides. Admission. (mid-April weekend)

EASTER EGG HUNT

MW – Pine Mountain. Wild Animal Safari. (800) 367-2751 or **www.animalsafari.com**. The site celebrates Easter with their annual Easter egg hunt (kids ages 3-9) with live animals or Gift Shop Certificates awarded as Grand Prizes. Admission. (Easter weekend)

EASTER EGGSTRAVAGANZA

MW – Pine Mountain. Callaway Gardens. (800) 225-5292 or **www.callawayonline.com**. Wear your favorite bonnet or Easter sweater and head out in the gardens for egg hunting. Admission. (Easter weekend)

April & Easter Events *(cont.)*

EGGSTRAVAGANZA

MW – The Rock. The Rock Ranch. 5020 Barnesville Hwy. (706) 647-6374 or **www.therockranch.com/Easter.htm**. Hundreds show up for a day of hunting eggs, visiting with the Easter bunny and reflecting on the true meaning of the season. The egg hunt begins at 1:00pm. There is a farmland petting zoo too. (Saturday before Easter Weekend)

BATTLE OF WEST POINT

MW – West Point. Fort Tyler (I-85, west on US 29). The annual commemoration of the April 16, 1865, Battle of West Point is held at the reconstructed Fort Tyler off Sixth Avenue. Living history demonstrations ending with a candlelight memorial service. FREE. (mid-April weekend)

GEORGIA RENAISSANCE FESTIVAL

NE – Fairburn. I-85 exit 61 @ Fairburn/Peachtree City. (770) 964-8575 or **www.georgiarenaissancefestival.com**. Enter the gates of elaborate 15th Century Kingdom and you'll be welcomed by over 1,000 colorfully costumed characters on twelve stages packed with great shows, a jousting tournament, a medieval amusement park, and Birds of Prey Show. Feast like a king on an enormous roasted turkey leg or other hand-held foods. Admission. (Mid-April thru early June weekends, including Memorial Day)

WORLD'S LARGEST EASTER EGG HUNT

NE – Homer. Garrison Home. (800) 638-5004. FREE to the public, no age limit. (Easter Sunday)

RIVERFEST WEEKEND

MW – Columbus. Historic area. (706) 324-7417. Event featuring Salisbury Fair (crafts, carnival, food court), Pig Jig, and Folklife Village (display, sell, and demonstrate their talents, a Children's Interactive Art Area, Fine Crafts, and Native American Primitive Skills Demonstrators). Admission. (last full weekend in April)

PAN AFRICAN FESTIVAL

MW – Macon. Tubman African American Museum. (478) 743-8544 or **www.tubmanmuseum.com**. Event includes concerts, soul food, Pan African Parade Family Day @ Central City Park, Health Fair, and Children's Village. (third week of April)

SPRING FARM DAYS

NW – Canton. **www.caglesdairy.com/spring.htm**. Cagle's Dairy. Come out to Hickory Flat and learn about when farming was a way of life for most of our ancestors. Historic Trades Exhibits include craftsmen smithing, weaving and caning. Wagon rides and antique tractor show. Admission. (last weekend in April)

CELTIC AND HERITAGE FESTIVAL

NW – Dalton, Tunnel Hill (I-75 exit 336, Hwy 41 north). **www.tunnelhillceltic.org**. The festival highlights the Scottish and Cherokee influences on the area. (first or second weekend in April)

EASTER EGGSTRAVAGANZA

NW – Atlanta Area. Callanwolde Fine Arts Center. (866) 633-5252 or **www.callanwolde.org**. Callanwolde and Radio Disney present a giant Easter egg hunt, interactive games and activities, concessions, local personalities, music, Easter baskets, candy and prizes. (Saturday before Easter)

April & Easter Events *(cont.)*

EASTER SUNRISE SERVICE

NW – Stone Mountain. Top of Stone Mountain & Memorial Lawn. **www.stonemountainpark.com**. (800) 317-2006. The Stone Mountain Ministerial Association will present two simultaneous, non-denominational Easter services at the top of Stone Mountain and at the base of the mountain on Memorial Lawn. (Easter Sunday early morning)

EASTER BUNNY BREAKFAST CRUISE

SE – Savannah. River Street Riverboat. (800) 786-6404. Get ready for a hopping good time. The Easter Bunny will be on board during the cruise, with lots of activities and a yummy breakfast buffet. Admission. (Easter Sunday & weekend before)

ATTACK ON FORT PULASKI ANNIVERSARY

SE – Tybee Island, Fort Pulaski National Monument. (912) 786-5787. The siege and reduction weekend commemorates this event with demonstrations and ranger programs. (second weekend in April)

SPRING FESTIVAL

SW – Lumpkin. **www.westville.org**. View crop plantings with mules, as well as musicians playing traditional instruments and school children in period dress attending 1850s style classes complete with slate boards and pencils. (first two weeks of April)

SPRING FOLK LIFE FESTIVAL

SW – Tifton. Agrirama. **www.agrirama.com**. (229) 386-3344. Special demonstrations of the labors, including sheep shearing. rail spitting, log rolling, textile arts, quilting, workshops and more, plus enjoy music at the Wiregrass Opry. Special Antique Show & Turpentine Stilling. Admission. (Saturday of second weekend in April)

MAY

VIDALIA ONION FESTIVAL

ME – Vidalia. Downtown. **www.vidaliaga.com**. (912) 538-8687. Festival events include an air show, fireworks, a street dance, rodeo, onion-eating contest, etc. (first long weekend in May)

MOTHER'S DAY BRUNCH

NE – Dawsonville. Amicalola Falls State Park. (800) 573-9656. Mother's Day Brunch in the park's scenic restaurant includes a flower with Mom's meal, and kids can make a craft just for Mom. $2.00 parking, brunch cost. (Mothers Day)

MOTHER'S DAY SPECIAL

MW – Pine Mountain. Wild Animal Safari. (800) 367-2751 or **www.animalsafari.com**. All mothers' tickets are ½ price. (Mother's Day)

MULE DAY

NE – Jefferson. Shields Ethridge Heritage Farm. (706) 367-2949 or **www.shieldsethridgefarm.org**. Events are open to the public including demonstrations of traditional farm equipment and animals. The farm has a commissary, blacksmith shop, cotton gin, grist mill, wheat house, and many other historic farm buildings. (May)

BATTLE OF RESACA CIVIL WAR REENACTMENT

NW – Dalton, Resaca Confederate Cemetery (I-75 exit 333, Walnut Ave. east 2 miles, right on Thornton). (800) 331-3258 or **www.friendsofresaca.org**. Following the Battle of Resaca, this site became the burial place of 450 Confederates moved from shallow graves around the plantation home of Col. John Green. (third weekend in May)

May *(cont.)*

SCANDINAVIAN FESTIVAL, ATLANTA

NW – Marietta. Cobb Civic Center (I-75 exit 112). (770) 509-1649 or **www.scandga.org/festival**. Country House will be decorated to reflect images, scenes, products and specialties of Scandinavia. Each Scandinavian country will demonstrate their skills and dance. The Viking Group displays the dress and instruments that were used 1000 years ago. There is story telling, specialty foods, a marketplace, and children's room with games and creative activities. (first weekend in May)

BRUNSWICK SEAFOOD FESTIVAL

SE – Brunswick. Mary Ross Waterfront Park. (912) 265-4032. Fresh seafood prepared in every conceivable way, live entertainment, games for the kids, The Scrapyard Navy Boat Race (for kids at heart), The Brunswick Rotary Club Rubber Duck Race, art and crafts vendors, historic home tours, car, boat and industry displays, and special sales in the Historic Old Town National Register Historic District across the street from the park. (Mothers Day weekend)

SCOTTISH GAMES FESTIVAL

SE – Savannah. (912) 232-3945. A traditional-style Scottish Games festival featuring competitions, clan displays and booths, food and drink, music of the bagpipes & other Scottish music. (May)

SAND ARTS FESTIVAL, SCAD

SE – Tybee Island, North Beach. **www.scad.edu**. (912) 525-5225. This annual event invites sand-loving SCAD students to create forms in the sand on the beach. Four contests are available for viewing: sand castle, sand sculpture, sand relief and wind sculpture. (first Saturday in May)

COTTON PICKIN' FAIR

SW – Gay. (706) 538-6814 or **www.cpfair.com**. Share remnants of farm life on a festival ground dotted with sheds, farm buildings and a cotton gin from the early 1900s. The Logan Turnpike grist mill will turn out cornmeal and flour; the blacksmith will forge functional art work and Uncle Lonnie will share farm stories. The Royal Scottish Country Dancers and Bagpipers will lead visitors to music, dance, puppetry, and storytelling. Try baked, fried broiled, boiled, steamed and stewed tasty Southern foods. Admission. (first weekend of May and October)

1836 CREEK INDIAN WAR

SW – Lumpkin. Westville Village. **www.westville.org**. (888) 733-1850. Due to years of broken treaties and a new federal policy requiring the Indians to leave their native homes, Creek Indian tribes retaliated against settlers in 1836. Re-enactors in period clothing will portray soldiers assigned to protect local Westville citizens from Creek Indians as they attack the village. Horses, gun fighting, hand-to-hand combat and "wounded" people all add to the life-like skirmish. The event will give spectators a first hand, hair-raising account of what an Indian attack might have looked and felt like during that period of history. Admission. (Memorial Day weekend)

JUNE

FATHER'S DAY SPECIAL

MW – Pine Mountain. Wild Animal Safari. (800) 367-2751 or **www.animalsafari.com**. All Fathers' tickets are ½ price.

June *(cont.)*

OLD FARM DAYS FESTIVAL

MW – Woodland. Old South Farm Museum (Rte 1 Pleasant Valley Road, GA 41). See an assortment of tools, equipment, and household goods tracing Southern rural life from the 1800s to the 1960s. Experience the lifestyle of Americans before electricity. Pump water and wash clothes by hand. See a working smokehouse, grind grain, spin cotton, pack peaches, can veggies or press hay. (third weekend in June)

SCOTTISH FESTIVAL & HIGHLAND GAMES

NE – Blairsville. Meeks Park. (706) 745-5789 or **www.blairsvillescottishfestival.org**. Catch the excitement of clan gatherings, Scottish vendors, pipe and drum bands, parade of Tartans, athletics, border collie demonstrations, children's games, Scottish dancing and music in the village. Admission. (second weekend in June)

FATHER'S DAY

NE – Dawsonville. Amicalola Falls State Park. (800) 573-9656. Don't make Dad man the grill this Father's Day. Bring him to the park for food, fun and fishing, including barbeque, a horseshoe tournament, watermelon seed-spitting contest, and keepsake crafts made by the kids. $2.00 parking. (Father's Day)

MAGNOLIA STORYTELLING FESTIVAL

NW – Atlanta (Roswell). Bulloch Hall. (800) 776-7935 or **www.cvb.roswell.ga.us**. Talented storytellers, musicians, and interpreters gather in Roswell to share their stories. Friday morning is focused on "Children's Tales" (best time for them as most other performances are geared more to the adult audience). Down-home southern style food and marketplace gifts offered. (mid-June weekend)

NATIVE AMERICAN FESTIVAL

NW – Douglasville. Sweetwater Creek State Park. (770) 947-5920. Ceremonial stomp dance performances, authentic arts & crafts, storytelling, music, and native cuisine. (third Saturday in June)

JULY

WATERMELON DAYS FESTIVAL

MW – Cordele. (229) 273-1668. As the "Watermelon Capital of the World," Cordele naturally celebrates the quality and abundance of this locally grown fruit. Dancing, singing, parade, eat tons of watermelon, and competitions in seed-spitting contests. (two weeks in July)

GEORGIA MOUNTAIN FAIR

NE – Hiawassee. Georgia Mountains Fairgrounds. (706) 896-4191 or **www.georgia-mountain-fair.com**. The Exhibit Hall is open daily with exhibits, antique machinery and area information from the Forest Service, 4-H, etc. Country music and gospel concerts. Admission. (last eleven days of July)

JULY 4TH CELEBRATIONS

Celebrations of our nation's Birthday featuring live music, exhibits, concessions and fireworks.

- ❑ **ME – Augusta**. River Blast. River Walk/Augusta Common. (800) 726-0243 or **www.augustaga.org**. Activities include musical entertainment, dance, patriotic concert, cannon firing and fireworks display.
- ❑ **ME – Statesboro**. Firecracker Festival. Mill Creek Regional Park. (800) 568-3301.
- ❑ **MW – Juliette**. Jarrell Plantation Historic Site. (478) 986-5172. This celebration features a noon reading of the Declaration of Independence followed by three-legged races, sack races, and bygone crafts and chores. Admission.

July 4th Celebrations *(cont.)*

- ❑ **MW – Pine Mountain**. Callaway. Surf & Sand Spectacular. (800) 225-5292.
- ❑ **MW – Thomaston**. The Rock Ranch. (706) 647-9686 or **www.therockranch.com**.
- ❑ MW – Warm Springs. Roosevelt's Little White House. **www.fdr-littlewhitehouse.org**.
- ❑ **NE – Athens**. Bishop Park. Star Spangled classic. (800) 653-0603.
- ❑ **NE – Blairsville**. Vogel State Park. (706) 745-2628. Celebrate with a flag-raising ceremony, bicycle parade, paddle boat races, sandcastle building and watermelon eating contests, sack races, egg tosses and greased pole climb. $2.00 parking.
- ❑ **NE – Blue Ridge**. Downtown. (800) 899-6867. Fireworks and Old Timer's Day Celebration & Parade.
- ❑ **NE – Dahlonega**. (800) 231-5543. Downtown.
- ❑ **NE – Dawsonville**. All-American Happy Daze. Amicalola Falls State Park. (800) 573-9656. This weekend is filled with old-fashioned games, patriotic crafts, watermelon seed spitting contest, pie-eating contest, greased pole climb, Hula Hoop contests, hayrides and more. Each day ends with a nostalgic visit back to the '50s as the park's restaurant transforms into the Amicalola Diner. $2.00 parking. (three days around July 4th)
- ❑ **NE – Helen**. July 4th Mountain Style. Downtown. (800) 858-8027. BBQ, Band and Fireworks.
- ❑ **NW – Atlanta**. Peachtree Street Downtown. (404) 897-7385 or **www.argonneparades.com**. Salute 2 American Parade.

- ❑ **NW – Cartersville**. Red Top Mountain State Park and Lodge. (770) 975-4226. enjoy the lakeside beach or go on a guided hike. Nature programs, a bluegrass concert, fireworks & more. $2.00 parking.
- ❑ **NW – Conyers**. Georgia International Horse Park. (800) 266-9377
- ❑ **NW – Stone Mountain Park**. Fantastic Fourth Celebration. (800) 317-2006 or **www.stonemountainpark.com**. Laser show with fireworks.
- ❑ **SE – Brunswick**. Mary Ross Waterfront Park. **www.goldenislearts.org**. Feature organized and supervised classic games like sack races, tug-of-wars, horseshoes, various ball games, hula-hoop contests and more. Players compete for prizes of delicious whole South Georgia watermelons.
- ❑ **SE – Darien**. Cannons Across the Marsh. Fort King George Historic Site. (912) 437-4779. Celebrate America's birthday at this coastal fort with cannon firings, living history tours, demonstrations and free watermelon. Admission.
- ❑ **SE – Douglas**. Downtown. **www.cityofdouglas.com**.
- ❑ **SE – Jekyll Island**. (877) 4Jekyll. Fireworks Extravaganza at the beach. Fireworks with sound track on the radio. Fun Zone. FREE.
- ❑ **SE – Savannah**. Fantastic Fourth Celebration. On the river. (912) 234-0295 or **www.savriverstreet.com**. (July 4th and day after)
- ❑ **SE – Savannah**. Fireworks Cruise, River Street Riverboat. (800) 786-6404 or **www.savannahriverboat.com**. Enjoy the spectacular fireworks from the water. Dance or sit back and relax. Admission. (8:00pm boarding, 9:00pm departure)

July 4th Celebrations *(cont.)*

- ❑ **SE – Savannah**. Tribute to the American Soldier. Old Fort Jackson. (912) 651-6895 or **www.chsgeorgia.org**. Celebrate with soldiers representing America's Army through the ages. The American Revolution, War of 1812 and Civil War will be represented. Cannon firing and musket firing demonstrations will be conducted throughout the weekend. (Independence Day weekend)
- ❑ **SE – St. Mary's**. Downtown. (800) 868-8687.
- ❑ **SE – Tybee Island**. Fireworks on the south end beach. (912) 224-2330 or **www.tybeevisit.com**.
- ❑ **SW – Cordele**. Downtown. (229) 273-1668. Fireworks Extravaganza.
- ❑ **SW – Cordele**. Georgia Veterans State Park. (229) 276-2371. A fireworks show will kick off Friday and old-fashioned games will be held on Saturday. Whole weekend features hayrides, historical tours and nature crafts. $2.00 parking.
- ❑ **SW – Lumpkin**. **www.westville.org**. Barbeque, games such as the grease-pole climb, and blowing-sky-high of the blacksmith's buried anvil.
- ❑ **SW – Tifton**. Agrirama. (229) 386-3344. Old Fashioned July 4th Celebration.

AUGUST

FAMILY FISHING FESTIVAL

SE – Jekyll Island. Pier at Clam Creek Picnic Area. (877) 4-JEKYLL. Fishing, goody bags, lunch and a ticket to Summer Waves Water Park. Registration required. FREE. (last Saturday in August)

SEPTEMBER

BARNESVILLE BUGGY DAYS

MW – Barnesville, Main Street, downtown. (770) 358-5884 or **www.barnesville.org**. The annual festival features a parade of buggies, equestrian units, antique cars and floats. Entertainment includes old-fashioned games, a car show, a military band, fireworks, music and dancers. In Buggy Blast Fun Park, kids can try a variety of fun activities. (third week in September)

GEORGIA STATE FAIR

MW - Macon. Central City Park. (800) 768-3401 or **www.georgiastatefair.org**. Games, carnival, fair food, Animal Magic Shows, Wildlife Educational Shows, Duck Races, Reptile Shows, Hillbilly Comedy Shows, contests, and livestock exhibits and competitions. Admission. (third week of September)

OCMULGEE INDIAN CELEBRATION

MW – Macon. Ocmulgee National Monument Indian Mounds. (478) 752-8257 or **www.nps.gov/acmu**. America's first music makers, Native Americans representing at least five different Nations (Creek, Choctaw, Chickasaw, Cherokee and Seminole), return to the place where man first sat down to celebrate their heritage. Ceremonial stomp dance performances, authentic arts & crafts, storytelling, music, and native cuisine. Picnics welcome. Admission. (third weekend in September)

SKY HIGH HOT AIR BALLOON FESTIVAL

MW – Pine Mountain. Callaway. (800) CALLAWAY. Hot air balloons fill the sky. Balloon Glow on Friday night. Family activities include tethered balloons, helicopter rides, line dancing, and live entertainment. (Labor Day weekend)

September *(cont.)*

SCULL SHOALS FESTIVAL

NE – Greensboro. Scull Shoals, Chattahoochee-Oconee National Forest, Macedonia Church Road. (800) 886-5253 or **www.fs.fed.us/conf/sculfrnd.htm**. Scull Shoals is an extinct town on the Oconee River, site of a 19th century mill village which included Georgia's first paper mill. The 2,200 acre experimental forest area, containing the mill town, a prehistoric mound complex dating from 1250-1500 AD, and beaver ponds and streams along the Oconee River. Archeological digs and old-fashioned food and games. (September)

APPLE PICKIN' JUBILEE

NW – Ellijay. Hillcrest Orchards, 9696 Hwy 52 East (9 miles east of town). (706) 273-3888. Pick your own apples or buy some apples and apple products in Grandma's Kitchen. Large picture windows allow you to watch them cooking. The barn is bursting with baby farm animals and a winding trail leads you through the forest filled with scenes from Fairy Tales and Nursery Rhymes. Meet Barney the Talking Bull or the giant Man Eating Catfish aboard one the their tractor-drawn wagons as it travels the orchards laden with apples headed for the "Land of Oz". The wagon goes through the water and below Rainbow Mountain. There are honey bee demos, a pig race, pedal cart track racing & apple bobbing. Admission. (last two weekends in September)

BATTLE OF TUNNEL HILL REENACTMENT

NW – Dalton. Tunnel Hill behind Meadowlawn. Tunnel Hill Heritage Center. (800) 331-3258. General William Sherman took over Meadowlawn while planning his Atlanta campaign. The battle is reenacted to memorialize the heritage and courage of those who fought in our country's most tragic war. (weekend after Labor Day)

PLAINS PEANUT FESTIVAL

SW – Plains. (229) 824-5373 or **www.plainsgeorgia.com**. Continuous free entertainment, historical and educational displays, recipe contests, and food. President Jimmy Carter will present awards for events. The Carters will also be available for a book signing early afternoon. President Carter and the Secret Service battle the Plains High School alumni at their annual softball game on Sunday. The SAM Shortline Excursion Train with vintage cars, will run shuttles all afternoon. At the Recipe Contest, a pro chef will prepare the winning recipes and offer samples of the peanut dishes. The Plains musical folk play " If the Sidewalks Could Talk," will be performed at the high school in the evening. (last weekend in September)

SEPTEMBER / OCTOBER

CORN MAZE

MW – The Rock. The Rock Ranch. 5020 Barnesville Hwy. (706) 647-6374 or **www.therockranch.com/maze.htm**. Each year the Rock contracts a pro maze company to help you get lost in a corn maze. Don't worry about the maze being too difficult, they have trained employees stationed in observation towers to help. (early September thru October)

FALL AT BURT'S FARM

NE – Dawsonville. Burt's Farm (4801 Highway 52). (800) 600-BURT or **www.burtsfarm.com**. Come out to the fall foliage in a sea of orange created by thousands of Burt's pumpkins. They offer hayrides and field trips pulled by John Deere tractors that take you through a winding trail filled with nature and beauty. Stop at the Pumpkin House to hear Autumn and Gourdy…the talking pumpkins. The hayride ends hilltop with a view of Amicalola. Admission. (weekends mid-September to mid November)

September / October *(cont.)*

UNCLE SHUCK'S CORN MAZE AND PUMPKIN PATCH

NE – Dawsonville. Uncle Shuck's (I-295 exit GA 400 north to GA 53). (888) OSHUCKS. Admission. (Labor Day weekend thru long weekends in October)

MAIZE

NW – Canton. **www.caglesdairy.com/MaiZE3.htm**. Cagle's Dairy. The Cagle family and a leading maze designer hope to challenge the wits of those seeking to find the one exit from their mind-boggling puzzle. Though the correct pathway can be walked in 45 minutes, most wanderers will require about one hour to travel more than three miles of twists, turns, and decision points. Enjoy the dairy tour, good farm food, and the option for small children to ride the Cow Wagon Train through the corn stalks. Admission. (weekends Labor Day through third weekend in November, Friday-Sunday)

NORTH GEORGIA STATE FAIR

NW – Marietta. Jim Miller Park (I-75 exit 260 west). (770) 423-1330 or **www.northgeorgiastatefair.com**. Start with fair food, amusement rides, to top entertainment concerts. Then add in animal shows and the Human Cannon Ball who is shot across the entire midway several times per day. Admission. (end of September to first week in October)

OCTOBER

OSSAHATCHEE INDIAN FESTIVAL AND POW-WOW

MW – Hamilton. Harris County Soccer Field, GA 116E. **www.ossahatchee.org**. You will witness American Indian dances and stories that have been passed down through the ages. Taste authentic American Indian Foods. Vendors from all over the United States will display and sell American Indian Arts and Crafts from artwork to pottery to intricately designed jewelry and leather goods. Primitive Skills from basket weaving to primitive weapons construction will be demonstrated by some of the most highly skilled artisans in North America. Admission. (third weekend in October)

MOSSY CREEK BARNYARD FESTIVAL

MW – Perry-Warner Robins. Deep Piney Woods (6 miles east of I-75, exit 138, Thompson Road). (478) 922-8265 or **www.mossycreekfestival.com**. Step into an enchanted forest full of Appalachian mountain music, hammered dulcimer, folk songs, Fantasy Forest storytelling, and Ragtime piano. Watch wood-carving, weaving and handbuilding fishing rods. There is also animal petting areas and hayrides. Admission. (mid-October weekend)

GREAT PUMPKIN PATCH

MW – Pine Mountain. First United Methodist Church. 208 McDougald Avenue. (706) 663-2538. Come down to the Pumpkin Patch for pumpkins, food, storytelling, face painting, hayrides, music, crafts, and homemade baked items. (afternoon to dusk, daily - last two weeks in October)

HARVEST FESTIVAL

MW – Pine Mountain. Callaway Gardens. (706) 663-5153 or **www.callawayonline.com**. Mr. Cason's Vegetable Garden is a bushel of fun for everyone. Basket weavers, quilters, storytelling, apple bobbing, and making your own corn-shuck dolls are just some of the creative activities that fill this festival. Scarecrow Contest. (weekends in October)

October *(cont.)*

PUMPKINS, PUMPKINS, PUMPKINS

NE – Blairsville. Southern Tree Plantation (4.7 miles south of town). **www.southerntreeplantation.com**. (706) 745-0601. Hayrides, kids train ride, petting farm, maze, marshmallow roasting, pony rides and inflatable slides. Admission. (weekends – Friday thru Sunday in October)

SORGHUM FESTIVAL

NE – Blairsville. (706) 745-4745 or (877) 745-5789. Celebrating the lost art of sorghum syrup-making, the festival will have live demonstrations showing how the cane is crushed and cooked as well as jars of the sweet syrup for sale. Participate in contests such as Bisket Eatin', Pole Climbin", Syrup Soppin', Rock Throwin", Horseshoe Throwin", and Log Sawin". There's also live country music, singing, square dancing, and a Sorghum Parade and Car Show. (three full weekends in October)

GEORGIA MOUNTAIN FALL FESTIVAL

NE – Hiawassee. (706) 896-4191 or **www.georgia-mountain-fair.com**. Includes arts and crafts, kiddie rides, demos by craftsmen (board splitting, blacksmithing, quilting, corn milling, shake making, cider squeezing, soap making). Visitors can tour the Pioneer Village, a replica of an old mountain town with a mercantile store, one room schoolhouse, log home, smokehouse, barn, and corncrib. Watch country and gospel singing, clogging or attend the Georgia State Fiddlers convention. Admission. (second full week of October)

GREAT LOCOMOTIVE CHASE FESTIVAL

NW – Adairsville. Downtown Square (I-75 exit 306). (800) 733-2280. Arts and crafts festival in the town that witnesses Andrews' Raiders Civil War escapade. Today the entire town is on the National Register of Historic Places. Enjoy crafts, artwork, entertainment, food and parade with fireworks in the evening. Street dancing on Friday & Saturday evenings; Gospel singing Sunday. Admission. (first weekend in October)

ATLANTA GREEK FESTIVAL

NW – Atlanta. Greek Orthodox Cathedral of the Annunciation. **www.atlgoc.org/festival.htm**. Celebrate Greek heritage with music, dancing, singing and mouthwatering food. (sccond weekend in October)

SCARECROWS IN THE GARDEN

NW – Atlanta. Botanical Garden. (404) 876-5859. Imaginative scarecrows on display in the Children's garden. Special activities are scheduled every weekend in October from 1-4:00pm. Children of all ages are welcome to come and enjoy a fun-filled day of activities that include the following: Face Painting, Make a scarecrow puppet, Make a spider magnet, Craft corn activity, and Make a scarecrow bookmark. Admission. (month-long in October)

BATTLE OF ALLATOONA PASS ENCAMPMENT

NW – Cartersville. Battlefield (I-75 exit 283). (800) 733-2280 or **www.notatlanta.org**. Visit with Civil War soldiers near the field hospital that still bears bullet holes (home open for tours). Fought on October 5, 1864, this battle was the inspiration for the familiar hymn "Hold the Fort," and is remembered for the summons to surrender message by a Confederate General, "in order to avoid a needless effusion of blood." (October weekend)

October *(cont.)*

ETOWAH VALLEY INDIAN FESTIVAL

NW – Cartersville. Friendship Plaza, Downtown (I-75 exit 288). (800) 733-2280. Celebrating Cartersville's rich Native American heritage with traditional dance, music, foods, storytelling and educators of traditional crafts and survival skills. Sponsored by the City of Cartersville, the festival is part of a month-long "Cowboys and Indians in Cartersville" extravaganza surrounding Booth Western Art Museum. FREE. (second weekend in October)

PUMPKIN PATCH

NW – Cartersville. Pettit Creek Farms (I-75 exit 288). (770) 386-8688. Arts & crafts, demonstrations, live music, food court, petting zoo, moonwalks, corn maize, pony rides, animals, pumpkin pickin' patch. Admission (age 10+). (second weekend in October)

PRATER'S MILL COUNTRY FAIR

NW – Dalton (Varnell). Prater's Mill, GA Hwy 2 (I-75 exit 341, north on Hwy 201 to Hwy 2, left 2.6 miles to the mill). (706) 694-6455 or **www.pratersmill.org**. Self-guided tours of Prater's Mill, Shugart Cotton Gin, 1898 Prater's Store and Westbook Barn; Civil War living history; nature trail; canoeing; pony rides; and barn animals. The 1855 water-powered gristmill still grinds corn and wheat the old-fashioned way. This is also the site of Union and Confederate troops during the Civil War. Southern foods, mountain music, square dancing, and storytelling. Admission. (Columbus Day Weekend, each October)

BATTLE OF JONESBORO REENACTMENT

NW – Jonesboro. Stately Oaks Plantation. (770) 473-0197. This 1839 planter's home, nestled among live oaks is the site for a day of costumed interpreters and battle re-enactments. Admission. (second weekend in October)

GEORGIA APPLE FESTIVAL

NW – Ellijay. Fairgrounds. **www.geogiaapplefestival.com**. (706) 635-7400. Producing 500,000 bushels of apples each fall, Gilmer County is Georgia's Apple Capital. Great food, a children's section, live entertainment, a parade, and hand-made country products. (second and third weekend in October)

PUMPKINS IN THE VALLEY FALL FESTIVAL

NW – Powder Springs. www.sunvalleybeach.com. Sun Valley Beach. Challenging maze, pumpkin patch, hay rides, games, food, and entertainment. Admission. (Saturday in mid-October)

PUMPKIN FESTIVAL

NW – Stone Mountain. www.stonemountainpark.com. (800) 317-2006. Celebrate fall in Crossroads with pumpkin and fall decorations, The Pumpkin Pyramid – The South's Largest Talking Pumpkin Tree, a hay maze, fall treats and great live entertainment. Guests of all ages can participate in a variety of activities, arts & crafts and contests. (weekends in October)

STONE MOUNTAIN HIGHLAND GAMES

NW – Stone Mountain. www.stonemountainpark.com. (800) 317-2006. Experience two days of great fun with Highland athletic events, dancing, piping, drumming, and Scottish Harping. Join in for Scottish country dancing demonstrations, Kirking of the Tartans, Clan Challenge, and the Parade of the Tartans. See the Clan and Tartan information tents along with many colorful Scottish shops. Rain or shine. (third weekend in October)

October *(cont.)*

PARADISE PASTURES PUMPKIN PATCH

NW – Taylorsville. Paradise Pastures Farm & Petting Zoo. 650 Taylorsville Macedonia Road (I-75 exit 288, GA 113 south, west on Euharlee 9.5 miles). (770) 382-4119 or **www.paradisepastures.com**. Bring the family and friends and enjoy daily hayrides, spooky nighttime hay ride, a large petting zoo featuring kangaroos and lots of baby animals, a play area for kids with inflatables, and a nightly bonfire. Food & refreshments available for purchase. Admission. Call for field trip and group rates. (Daily in October thru first week of November)

HARVEST FESTIVAL

SW – Lumpkin. 1 MLK Drive. **www.westville.org**. When the leaves change color, this town celebrates harvest time with music and crafts, sugar syrup and cotton gin operation. (early October thru early November)

GEORGIA NATIONAL FAIR

SW – Perry. Georgia National Fairgrounds & Agricenter (I-75 exit 134 & 135). (478) 987-3247 or **www.gnfa.com**. A celebration of Georgia's youth, agriculture, and heritage with competitive exhibits, food, midway rides and games, vendors, street entertainers, free family entertainment, free circus, nightly fireworks, and major concerts. The Georgia National Schoolhouse attracts pre-K through high school students to tour the educational exhibits with students admitted free. Admission for adults. Kids FREE. (nine days in early October)

NOVEMBER

SYRUP MAKIN' & STORYTELLIN'

MW – Juliette. Jarrell Plantation. (478) 986-5172. **www.mylink.net/~jarrell**. The traditional syrup cookoff was an important fall event on middle Georgia farms and featured family and community getting together for work and play. This program brings this event back to life with demonstrations of the sugar cane mill, syrup kettle, steam engine, woodstove cooking, and also storytelling. Admission. (second weekend in November)

BABYLAND'S APPALACHIAN CHRISTMAS

NE – Cleveland. www.cabbagepatchkids.com. Babyland General Hospital. (weekend before Thanksgiving)

POW WOW & INDIAN FESTIVAL

NW – Stone Mountain. www.stonemountainpark.com. (800) 317-2006. Celebrate the history and heritage of native peoples through education and entertainment. Native Americans from across the United States will gather to compete in dance and drum competitions. Primitive skills educators will demonstrate fire making, basket weaving, hide tanning and will prepare Native American foods. Native arts and crafts will be available for purchase and the kids will love the live buffalo, bear and other animals. (first weekend in November)

NOVEMBER / DECEMBER

CHRISTMAS AROUND THE WORLD

MW – Americus. Habitat's Global Village & Discovery Center. (866) 924-5823 or **www.habitat.org/gvdc**. Tour international homes decorated for the Christmas holiday and learn about traditions and practices from around the world. Included is an exhibit of international dolls and their currency or similar multi-cultural exhibit. Admission. (Thanksgiving weekend through December)

CHRISTMAS AT HAY HOUSE

MW – Macon. Hay House. 934 Georgia Avenue. **www.hayhouse.org**. The tradition of grand holiday decorating continues today. In addition to tours of the historic home decorated for the holiday season, special events are offered such as children's Victorian Christmas parties, catered lunches in the house museums including the House, the Cannonball House, and the Sidney Lanier Cottage. A special program book designed for the Christmas season is distributed to guests throughout the month. Admission. (December)

FANTASY IN LIGHTS

MW – Pine Mountain. Callaway Gardens. (800) CALLAWAY or **www.callawayonline.com**. Celebrate the shining glory of the holiday season with one of the world's largest light and sound shows. Advance tickets required. (Mid-November thru December)

CHRISTMAS EXPRESS

NE – Blue Ridge. Scenic Railway. **www.brscenic.com**. (800) 934-1898. Treat your family to an old-fashioned Christmas singing carols, listening to the story of the Polar Express, and visiting with Santa and his elves. Admission. (weekends third week of November thru third weekend in December)

COCOA AND CANDLES / LIGHT UP DUNWOODY

NW – Atlanta (Dunwoody). Dunwoody Nature Center. **www.dunwoodynature.org/cocoacandles.html**. The Village is all a-twinkle with a fairyland of luminaries lining the trails and boardwalk. Make a holiday natural wreath and enjoy some cocoa. (Sunday after Thanksgiving for one week)

PETTIT CREEK CHRISTMAS HOLIDAY LIGHTS DISPLAY

NW – Cartersville. Pettit Creek Farms (I-75 exit 288 west). (770) 386-8688. Christmas light show extravaganza open nightly. Hayrides through the lights nightly – bring your lap blanket. Christmas tree and wreath sales. Buy a tree and see the lights for free. Admission. (end of November thru end of December)

SOUTHERN CHRISTMAS / STONE MOUNTAIN PARK

NW – Stone Mountain. **www.stonemountainpark.com**. (800) 317-2006. The magic of a small town Christmas comes alive for the whole family during A Southern Christmas. The 1870s town of Crossroads is filled with fascinating townsfolk, entertainers and skilled crafters. The town will be decorated with millions of Christmas lights, creating a charming & magical atmosphere. Families will enjoy the live entertainment, the 4D Christmas Movie – Tinker Doodle, train ride with a live show and visiting Santa Claus. Guests can find the perfect gifts at many unique shops and enjoy home-cooked Southern fare and holiday treats at a wide variety of restaurants. (mid-November thru December)

SOUTHERN CHRISTMAS CAROL

SW – Colquitt. Swamp Gravy Playhouse. (229) 758-5450 or **www.swampgravy.com/christmas.html**. The folks who bring you Swamp Gravy Folk Play bring a southern-based version of classical Christmas drama. Admission. (day after Thanksgiving thru mid-December)

November / December *(cont.)*

CHRISTMAS WONDERLAND

SW – Valdosta. Wild Adventures Theme Park. (229) 219-7080 or **www.wildadventures.net**. The south's largest Christmas celebration, it features millions of beautiful lights, displays, sounds, and wonderful holiday shows including an ice skating spectacular "Christmas on Ice." Admission. (mid-November thru December)

DECEMBER

CHRISTMAS IN THE GARDENS

ME – Metter. Guido Gardens, 600 N. Lewis Street (GA 121 North). One million lights burning bright. Flying angels over the manger scene, animated Fishermen and Butterflies, and Noah and the ark. Enjoy this walk-through experience celebrating the beauty and wonder of Christmas. (nightly, entire month of December)

CHRISTMAS CANDLELIGHT TOUR

MW – Juliette. Jarrell Plantation Historic Site. (478) 986-5172. Tour this plantation by luminary and candlelight, then enjoy a campfire, carols, and Christmas stories from long ago. Admission. (second weekend in December)

CHRISTMAS AT CALLAWAY

MW – Pine Mountain. Callaway Plantation. (706) 678-7060. Experience Christmas décor and activities of the Old South. (first weekend in December)

CHRISTMAS PROGRAM AT FDR'S LITTLE WHITE HOUSE

MW – Warm Springs. FDR's Little White House. (706) 655-5780. Christmas readings by FDR and Eleanor in a living room setting of the 1930s with Santa and other Christmas activities. (mid-December afternoon)

CHRISTMAS OPEN HOUSE

NE – Dawsonville. Amicalola Falls State Park. (706) 265-4703 or **www.gastateparks.org/info/amicalola**. Visit with Santa and enjoy choir performances, hayrides, artwork by local children and gingerbread displays. A holiday buffet will be served in the park's restaurant. Some fees. (second weekend in December)

FIRST NIGHT GAINESVILLE

NE – Gainesville. Downtown Square. (888) 536-0005. First Night is a family-oriented non-alcoholic celebration of the arts held each year on New Year's Eve. First Night begins with a Children's Festival featuring magic shows, puppets, and crafts. Children help build large puppets which are later carried in the First Night Procession around the Gainesville Square. Following the Children's Festival, families are invited to enjoy indoor performances of all kinds including; Country, Rock, Jazz, Irish Folk, Magic, and more. The grand finale begins at 11:30pm around the Main Stage on the downtown square. At midnight, thousands of people ring in the New Year with Northeast Georgia's largest fireworks show. Admission buttons. (December 31st, New Years Eve)

DECK THE HALLS

NE – Helen. Unicoi State Park and Lodge. (800) 573-9659. This holiday celebration includes making holiday crafts, hayrides and an evening of music. Festival of trees. $2.00 parking. (first two weeks of December)

December *(cont.)*

ATLANTA CHRISTMAS PARADE & FESTIVAL OF TREES

NW – Atlanta. Georgia World Congress Center. (404) 325-NOEL. Strike up the band! With each passing year, more and more children and families crowd the streets of Atlanta for a little holiday magic. Officially kick off the Festival of Trees! If you can't join the parade downtown, be sure to catch it on WSB-TV Channel 2. Pre-Parade coverage begins at 10:00am. FREE parade. (parade first Saturday in December, festival of trees lasts until mid-December)

HOLIDAY IN THE GARDEN

NW – Atlanta. Botanical Garden. (404) 876-5859. **www.atlantabotanicalgarden.org**. Activities and crafts for children and their families, along with live holiday performances and entertainment, will enliven the afternoon. And to celebrate the holidays, admission is free for all children 12 and under. Garden members enter free; regular admission rates apply for non-members over 12. Parking available at Colony Square ($2.00 per vehicle with voucher) with free shuttle service to the Garden. Held rain or shine. (first Sunday in December)

UNDERGROUND ATLANTA PEACH DROP

NW – Atlanta. Underground Atlanta. (404) 523-2311. **www.peachdrop.com**. Join in a day full of family fun and an evening full of top-notch entertainment. Beginning at noon on Thursday, December 31, Underground Atlanta will be bursting with activities for the entire family. Then, just before the clock strikes midnight, the New Year's Eve tradition will come alive when our 800-pound peach begins its descent! As the clock strikes 12 midnight, spectacular fireworks will fill the air. FREE. (New Years Eve)

CHRISTMAS FOR KIDS

NW – Atlanta (Roswell). Bulloch Hall. (770) 992-1731 or **www.bullochhall.org**. Yule log and candy cane hunt, make a Christmas craft, light snacks, and a visit from Mr. And Mrs. Claus. Or, watch the re-enactment of Mittie's 1853 Wedding as a family. Reservations. (second and third weekend in December)

CHRISTMAS AT THE CABIN

NW – Cartersville. Red Top Mountain State Park (I-75 exit 285). (770) 975-0055 or **www.gastateparks.org**. Join in an 1860's style Christmas celebration at the log cabin located behind the Lodge. Enjoy old-time Christmas music, open-hearth cooking, primitive toys, and chestnuts on the fire. Come early and have Breakfast with Santa at the Mountain Cove Restaurant. Pictures will be available. Early December, bring your family for dinner at the lodge and enjoy holiday craft activities for children. Local artisans will be on hand to help with your shopping. $2.00 park pass. (first two Saturdays in December)

CHRISTMAS BY CANDLELIGHT CHEROKEE HOME TOUR

NW – Chatsworth. Chief Vann House Historic Site. (706) 695-2598. Experience an 1800s Christmas in one of America's best preserved Cherokee Indian homes. Admission. (second weekend in December)

POSSUM DROP, THE

NW – Tallapoosa. (770) 574-7193. Forget Times Square and Atlanta's Ball Drop. Come to downtown Tallapoosa for the Possum Drop on New Year's Eve beginning at 11:30pm. Featuring live entertainment and fireworks display with breakfast to follow. (New Year's Eve)

December *(cont.)*

NEW YEAR'S EVE PARTY IN THE PARK

SE – Brunswick. **www.brunswickgeorgia.net**. (912) 265-4032. This New Years event features "The Giant Shrimp Drop" in which a nine-foot shrimp descends from a fifty-foot tower into a ten-foot high glass of cocktail sauce. When the shrimp hits the sauce, fireworks explode over Oglethorpe Bay to welcome in another year. (New Years Eve)

HOLIDAY ISLAND

SE – Jekyll Island History Center & Historic District. (912) 635-4036. Christmas Light Tours - Guides take you on an one-hour evening tram tour through the National Historic Landmark District in all its holiday splendor. Magical Night of Christmas Stories – The Jekyll Island Museum guides weave Christmas stories the first Saturday in December. Professional storytellers and refreshments. Bingo with Santa – Hot cocoa, punch and cupcakes. Santa calls the numbers for bingo at Villas by the Sea Resort. Admission. (weekends in December)

WINTER MUSTER AND CANDLELIT TOUR

SE – Richmond Hill. Fort McAllister Historic Park. (912) 727-2339. Experience Fort McAllister's fall to the Union army. Admission. (second Saturday in December)

CHRISTMAS ON THE RIVER

SE – Savannah. City Market, River Street and Savannah Harbor. (912) 232-4903. Bring the family to historic downtown for fun-filled activities including cookie decorating, making ornaments, cloggers, petting zoo with Father Christmas, and photos with Santa. Enjoy the kickoff of the Savannah Harbor Holiday series with a parade of more than 60 festively decorated yachts and sailboats followed by a fireworks extravaganza. (December weekends)

CHRISTMAS LIGHTS ON THE LAKE

SE – Waycross. Laura S. Walker State Park. (912) 287-4900. Enjoy carols, marshmallow roasting, games, a hayride through hundreds of lights, and a visit from Santa. Admission. (first Saturday in December)

YULETIDE SEASON

SW – Lumpkin. 1 MLK Drive. **www.westville.org**. Christmas Decorating Workshop, Yule Log Ceremony, Christmas Tree Lightings, and the Burning of the Greens Ceremony. (Saturdays in December)

1890's VICTORIAN CHRISTMAS CELEBRATION

SW – Tifton. Georgia Agrirama. (229) 386-0216. Enjoy Christmas in an 1890's rural south village with historic decorations, Christmas carolers, a live nativity scene & the famous dessert sampler. Children can visit with Santa and shop at the Secret Santa Shop. Admission. (second Saturday in December)

Master
Index

Activity Index

AMUSEMENTS

ANIMALS & FARMS

ANIMALS & FARMS (cont.)

HISTORY

HISTORY (cont.)

HISTORY (cont.)

MUSEUMS

MUSEUMS (cont.)

OUTDOOR EXPLORING

OUTDOOR EXPLORING (cont.)

OUTDOOR EXPLORING (cont.)

OUTDOOR EXPLORING (cont.)

SPORTS

THE ARTS

THE ARTS (cont.)

TOURS

TOURS (cont.)

Need more great ways to keep the kids busy?

www.KidsLoveTravel.com

Best-selling "Kids Love" Travel Guides now available for:

Georgia, Indiana, Kentucky, Michigan, North Carolina, Ohio Pennsylvania, Tennessee, and Virgina.

State Coloring Books:

Kids can color and learn new facts. Lots and fun and educational too. Includes State Characters, Places, Facts and Fun. Color your way around the state! All ages will enjoy these books. Various states.

State Big Activity Books:

Kids will learn about State History, Geography, People, Places, Nature, Animals, Holidays, Legend, Lore and much, much more by completing these enriching activities. Includes dot-to-dots, mazes, coloring, matching, word searches, riddles, crossword puzzles, word jumbles, writing, and many other creative activities. Each book is state specific fun! Reproducible. Grades 1-5. Correlates with State Academic Standards. Various states.

State Pocket Guides:

This handy easy-to-use guide is divided into 7 color coded sections (State Facts, Geography, History, People, Places, Nature, and more). Riddles, recipes, and surprising facts make this guide a delight. Various states.

Invisible Ink Book Sets:

(Includes special marker). Hours of "clean" fun for all. The special marker is clear so it doesn't make a mess. The invisible ink pen reveals invisibly printed pictures or answers to quizzes and games. What are you interested in? Sports ... Trivia ... History ... The Bible ... Fascinating Facts ... or just plain fun ...

(Just a sample of the many titles available below)

2 assorted titles (may vary from photo)

Travel Games:

ravel Bingo, Magnetic Paper Dolls Travel Tins, Magnetic ames in a CD case, etc.

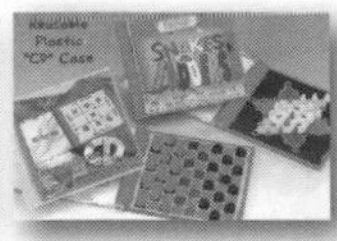

Kids Love Travel Memories!

Now that you've created memories with your family, it's time to keepsake them by scrapbooking in this unique, family-friendly way!

Step 1 - *Select, Cut, and Paste Your Favorite Travel Photos.*

Step 2 - *Color the Fun Theme Picture Frames.*

Step 3 - *Write About Your Travel Stories in the Journal (We get you started.)*

www.KidsLoveTravel.com

Travel Journal & Notes:

Travel Journal & Notes:

Travel Journal & Notes:

GROUP DISCOUNTS & FUNDRAISING OPPORTUNITIES!

We're excited to introduce our books to your group! These guides for parents, grandparents, teachers and visitors are great tools to help you discover hundreds of fun places to visit. Our titles are great resources for all the wonderful places to travel either locally or across the region.

We are two parents who have researched, written and published these books. We have spent thousands of hours collecting information and *personally traveled over 25,000 miles* visiting all of the most unique places listed in our guides. The books are kid-tested and the descriptions include great hints on what kids like best!

Please consider the following Group Purchase options: *For the latest information, visit our website:* **www.KidsLoveTravel.com**

- ❑ **Group Discount/Fundraising** – Purchase books at the discount price of $2.95 off the suggested retail price for members/friends. Minimum order is ten books. You may mix titles to reach the minimum order. Greater discounts (~35%) are available for fundraisers. Minimum order is thirty books. Call for details.

- ❑ **Available for Interview/Speaking** – The authors have a treasure bag full of souvenirs from favorite places. We'd love to share ideas on planning fun trips to take children while exploring your home state. The authors are available, by appointment, *(based on availability)* at (614) 792-6451 or **michele@kidslovepublications.com**. A modest honorarium or minimum group sale purchase will apply. Call or visit our website for details.

Call us soon at (614) 792-6451 to make arrangements!

Happy Exploring!

All titles are "Kid Tested". *The authors and kids personally visited all of the most unique places* and wrote the books with warmth and excitement from a parent's perspective. Listings provide: Names, addresses, telephone numbers, websites, directions, and descriptions. All books include a bonus chapter listing state-wide kid-friendly Seasonal & Special Events!

- ❑ **KIDS LOVE GEORGIA** - Explore hidden islands, humbling habitats, and historic gold mines. See playful puppets, dancing dolphins, and comical kangaroos. "Watch out" for cowboys, Indians, and swamp creatures. Over 500 listings in one book about Georgia travel. 6 geographical zones, 264 pages.
- ❑ **KIDS LOVE INDIANA** - Discover places where you can "co-star" in a cartoon or climb a giant sand dune. Over 500 listings in one book about Indiana travel. 8 geographical zones, 280 pages.
- ❑ **KIDS LOVE KENTUCKY** - Discover places from Boone to Burgoo, from Caves to Corvettes, and from Lincoln to the Lands of Horses. Nearly 500 listings in one book about Kentucky travel. 5 geographic zones. 186 pages.
- ❑ **KIDS LOVE MICHIGAN** - Discover places where you can "race" over giant sand dunes, climb aboard a lighthouse "ship", eat at the world's largest breakfast table, or watch yummy foods being made. Almost 600 listings in one book about Michigan travel. 8 geographical zones, 229 pages.
- ❑ **KIDS LOVE NORTH CAROLINA** - Explore places where you can "discover" gold and pirate history, explore castles and strange houses, or learn of the "lost colony" and Mayberry. Over 500 listings in one book about travel. 6 geographical zones, 288 pages.
- ❑ **KIDS LOVE OHIO** - Discover places like hidden castles and whistle factories. Over 800 listings in one book about Ohio travel. 9 geographical zones, 260 pages.
- ❑ **KIDS LOVE PENNSYLVANIA** - Explore places where you can "discover" oil and coal, meet Ben Franklin, or watch your favorite toys and delicious, fresh snacks being made. Over 900 listings in one book about Pennsylvania travel. 9 geographical zones, 268 pages.
- ❑ **KIDS LOVE TENNESSEE** – Explore places where you can "discover" pearls, ride the rails, "meet" Three Kings (of Rights, Rock & Soul). Be inspired to sing listening to the rich traditions of Country music fame. Over 500 listings in one book about Tennessee travel. 6 geographical zones, 235 pages.
- ❑ **KIDS LOVE THE VIRGINIAS** – Discover where ponies swim and dolphins dance, dig into archaeology and living history, or be dazzled by record-breaking and natural bridges. Over 900 listings in one book about Virginia & West Virginia travel. 8 geographical zones, 262 pages.

ORDER FORM

KIDS LOVE PUBLICATIONS

1985 Dina Court, Powell, Ohio 43065
(614) 792-6451
Visit our website: **www.KidsLoveTravel.com**

#	Title		Price	Total
	Kids Love Georgia		$14.95	
	Kids Love Indiana		$14.95	
	Kids Love Kentucky		$13.95	
	Kids Love Michigan		$13.95	
	Kids Love North Carolina		$14.95	
	Kids Love Ohio		$13.95	
	Kids Love Pennsylvania		$13.95	
	Kids Love Tennessee		$13.95	
	Kids Love the Virginias		$13.95	
	Kids Love Travel Memories!		$14.95	
	Combo Discount Pricing			
	Combo #2 - Any 2 Books		$26.95	
	Combo #3 - Any 3 Books		$37.95	
	Combo #4 - Any 4 Books		$47.95	
			Subtotal	
		(Ohio Residents Only – Your local rate)	Local/State Sales Tax	
		$2.00 first book $1.00 each additional	Shipping	
			TOTAL	

*(Please make check or money order payable to: **KIDS LOVE PUBLICATIONS**)*

☐ Master Card
☐ Visa

Account Number ☐☐☐☐-☐☐☐☐-☐☐☐☐-☐☐☐☐

Exp Date: ☐☐/☐☐ (Month/Year)

Cardholder's Name ______________________________

Signature *(required)* ______________________________

Name: ______________________________

Address: ______________________________

City: ____________________ State: ____________

Zip: ____________ Telephone: ______________

All orders are shipped within 2 business days of receipt by US Mail. If you wish to have your books autographed, please include a legible note with the message you'd like written in your book. Your satisfaction is 100% guaranteed or simply return your order for a prompt refund. Thanks for your order. Happy Exploring!

"Where to go?, What to do?, and How much will it cost?", are all questions that they have heard throughout the years from friends and family. These questions became the inspiration that motivated them to research, write and publish the "Kids Love" travel series.

This adventure of writing and publishing family travel books has taken them on a journey of experiences that they never could have imagined. They have appeared as guests on hundreds of radio and television shows, had featured articles in statewide newspapers and magazines, spoken to thousands of people at schools and conventions, and write monthly columns in many publications talking about "family friendly" places to travel.

George Zavatsky and Michele (Darrall) Zavatsky were raised in the Midwest and have lived in many different cities. They currently reside in a suburb of Columbus, Ohio. They feel very blessed to be able to create their own career that allows them to research, write and publish a series of best-selling kids' travel books. Besides the wonderful adventure of marriage, they place great importance on being loving parents to Jenny & Daniel.